William Shakespeare's
King John
In Plain and Simple English

BOOKCAPS

BookCaps Study Guides
www.bookcaps.com

© 2012. All Rights Reserved.

Table of Contents

About This Series 3
Characters 4
   Act I 6
      SCENE 1. 7
   Act II. 16
      SCENE 1. 17
   Act III. 36
      SCENE 1. 37
      SCENE 2. 48
      SCENE 3. 49
      SCENE 4. 52
   Act IV. 58
      SCENE 1. 59
      SCENE 2. 65
      SCENE 3. 74
   Act V 80
      SCENE 1. 81
      SCENE 2. 84
      SCENE 3. 89
      SCENE 4. 90
      SCENE 5. 92
      SCENE 6. 93
      SCENE 7. 95

About This Series

The "Classic Retold" series started as a way of telling classics for the modern reader—being careful to preserve the themes and integrity of the original. Whether you want to understand Shakespeare a little more or are trying to get a better grasps of the Greek classics, there is a book waiting for you!

Characters

KING JOHN
PRINCE HENRY, his son
ARTHUR, DUKE OF BRITAINE, son of Geffrey, late Duke of Britaine, the elder brother of King John
EARL OF PEMBROKE
EARL OF ESSEX
EARL OF SALISBURY
LORD BIGOT
HUBERT DE BURGH
ROBERT FAULCONBRIDGE, son to Sir Robert Faulconbridge
PHILIP THE BASTARD, his half-brother
JAMES GURNEY, servant to Lady Faulconbridge
PETER OF POMFRET, a prophet

KING PHILIP OF FRANCE
LEWIS, the Dauphin
LYMOGES, Duke of Austria
CARDINAL PANDULPH, the Pope's legate
MELUN, a French lord
CHATILLON, ambassador from France to King John

QUEEN ELINOR, widow of King Henry II and mother to King John
CONSTANCE, Mother to Arthur
BLANCH OF SPAIN, daughter to the King of Castile and niece to King John
LADY FAULCONBRIDGE, widow of Sir Robert Faulconbridge

Lords, Citizens of Angiers, Sheriff, Heralds, Officers, Soldiers, Executioners, Messengers, Attendants

SCENE:
England and France

Act I

SCENE 1

KING JOHN's palace

Enter KING JOHN, QUEEN ELINOR, PEMBROKE, ESSEX, SALISBURY, and others, with CHATILLON

KING JOHN.
Now, say, Chatillon, what would France with us?

Now tell me, Chatillon, what does the King of France want from me?

CHATILLON.
Thus, after greeting, speaks the King of France
In my behaviour to the majesty,
The borrowed majesty, of England here.

After the greeting this is what the King of France says, through me as his representative, to the counterfeit royalty of England.

ELINOR.
A strange beginning- 'borrowed majesty'!

This is a strange beginning—"counterfeit royalty"!

KING JOHN.
Silence, good mother; hear the embassy.

Quiet, good mother; listen to what it says.

CHATILLON.
Philip of France, in right and true behalf
Of thy deceased brother Geffrey's son,
Arthur Plantagenet, lays most lawful claim
To this fair island and the territories,
To Ireland, Poictiers, Anjou, Touraine, Maine,
Desiring thee to lay aside the sword
Which sways usurpingly these several titles,
And put the same into young Arthur's hand,
Thy nephew and right royal sovereign.

Philip of France, rightly and acting faithfully on behalf of the son of your dead brother Geoffrey, Arthur Plantagenet, makes a legally justified claim to this fair island and its dependencies, Ireland, Poitiers, Anjou, Touraine, Maine, asking you to withdraw the forces which falsely hold these titles, and to hand them over into the hands of young Arthur, your nephew and the true king.

KING JOHN.
What follows if we disallow of this?

What will happen if we disagree with this?

CHATILLON.
The proud control of fierce and bloody war,
To enforce these rights so forcibly withheld.

You will have to face a fierce and bloody war, for the return of these rights which you withhold by force.

KING JOHN.
Here have we war for war, and blood for blood,
Controlment for controlment- so answer France.

We can answer with war for war, blood for blood, force for force—tell France that.

CHATILLON.
Then take my king's defiance from my mouth-
The farthest limit of my embassy.

Then accept the defiance of the King from me— that's as far as my remit allows me.

KING JOHN.
Bear mine to him, and so depart in peace;

Take mine to him, and so leave peacefully;

Be thou as lightning in the eyes of France;
For ere thou canst report I will be there,
The thunder of my cannon shall be heard.
So hence! Be thou the trumpet of our wrath
And sullen presage of your own decay.
An honourable conduct let him have-
Pembroke, look to 't. Farewell, Chatillon.

you must be like lightning, warning France; because before you can speak to him I will be there, you shall hear the thunder of my cannons. So go! You can be the warning of my anger and the dismal announcer of your own downfall. Make sure he has a good escort— see to it, Pembroke. Farewell Chatillon.

Exeunt CHATILLON and PEMBROKE

ELINOR.
What now, my son! Have I not ever said
How that ambitious Constance would not cease
Till she had kindled France and all the world
Upon the right and party of her son?
This might have been prevented and made whole
With very easy arguments of love,
Which now the manage of two kingdoms must
With fearful bloody issue arbitrate.

What about that, my son! Haven't I always said that the ambitious Constance would not stop until she had France and the whole world fighting to support her son's rights and his followers? This could have been avoided and put right with very simple friendly behaviour, and now the question of who rules two kingdoms must be settled by terrible bloody war.

KING JOHN.
Our strong possession and our right for us!

We are in possession, and that means right is on our side!

ELINOR.
Your strong possession much more than your right,
Or else it must go wrong with you and me;
So much my conscience whispers in your ear,
Which none but heaven and you and I shall hear.

The strong grip you have is much more important than your rights, if it isn't, you and I will be in trouble; this is what I think deep down, but nobody but you and God will hear it.

Enter a SHERIFF

ESSEX.
My liege, here is the strangest controversy
Come from the country to be judg'd by you
That e'er I heard. Shall I produce the men?

My lord, I have here the strangest disagreement that I ever heard, with men come from the country to have your judgement. Shall I bring them in?

KING JOHN.
Let them approach.

Yes, bring them in.

Exit SHERIFF

Our abbeys and our priories shall pay
This expedition's charge.

The abbeys and the priories will pay for the cost of this war.

Enter ROBERT FAULCONBRIDGE and PHILIP, his bastard brother

What men are you?

Who are you?

BASTARD.

8

Your faithful subject I, a gentleman
Born in Northamptonshire, and eldest son,
As I suppose, to Robert Faulconbridge-
A soldier by the honour-giving hand
Of Coeur-de-lion knighted in the field.

KING JOHN.
What art thou?

ROBERT.
The son and heir to that same Faulconbridge.

KING JOHN.
Is that the elder, and art thou the heir?
You came not of one mother then, it seems.

BASTARD.
Most certain of one mother, mighty king-
That is well known- and, as I think, one father;
But for the certain knowledge of that truth
I put you o'er to heaven and to my mother.
Of that I doubt, as all men's children may.

ELINOR.
Out on thee, rude man! Thou dost shame thy mother,
And wound her honour with this diffidence.

BASTARD.
I, madam? No, I have no reason for it-
That is my brother's plea, and none of mine;
The which if he can prove, 'a pops me out
At least from fair five hundred pound a year.
Heaven guard my mother's honour and my land!

KING JOHN.
A good blunt fellow. Why, being younger born,
Doth he lay claim to thine inheritance?

BASTARD.
I know not why, except to get the land.
But once he slander'd me with bastardy;
But whe'er I be as true begot or no,
That still I lay upon my mother's head;
But that I am as well begot, my liege-
Fair fall the bones that took the pains for me!-
Compare our faces and be judge yourself.
If old Sir Robert did beget us both
And were our father, and this son like him-

*I am a faithful subject of yours, a gentleman
born in Northamptonshire, and the eldest son,
I believe, of Robert Faulconbridge–
a soldier who was knighted on the battlefield
by Richard the Lionheart.*

And who are you?

I am the son and heir of that same Faulconbridge.

*He's older than you, and you are the heir?
So it seems you don't have the same mother.*

*We certainly share the same mother, mighty King–
that is well known–and, I think, the same father;
but to have that proved for certain
you would have to ask heaven and my mother.
I have doubts about that, as any person may.*

*Damn you, rude man! You are shaming your mother,
and insulting her honour with these doubts.*

*Me, madam? No, I have no reason to do it;
that is what my brother says, not me;
if he can prove it he deprives me
of at least five hundred pounds a year.
May heaven protect the honour of my mother and
my property!*

*A good straightforward chap. Why, as he is the
younger, does he claim your inheritance?*

*I don't know why, except that he wants the land.
He did once slander me by calling a bastard;
but whether I am legitimately born or not
I leave to the evidence of my mother;
but that I am nobly born, my lord–
may good come to those who created me!–
Compare our faces and judge for yourself.
If Sir Robert created us both
and was our father, and this son is like him,*

O old Sir Robert, father, on my knee
I give heaven thanks I was not like to thee!

KING JOHN.
Why, what a madcap hath heaven lent us here!

ELINOR.
He hath a trick of Coeur-de-lion's face;
The accent of his tongue affecteth him.
Do you not read some tokens of my son
In the large composition of this man?

KING JOHN.
Mine eye hath well examined his parts
And finds them perfect Richard. Sirrah, speak,
What doth move you to claim your brother's land?

BASTARD.
Because he hath a half-face, like my father.
With half that face would he have all my land:
A half-fac'd groat five hundred pound a year!

ROBERT.
My gracious liege, when that my father liv'd,
Your brother did employ my father much-

BASTARD.
Well, sir, by this you cannot get my land:
Your tale must be how he employ'd my mother.

ROBERT.
And once dispatch'd him in an embassy
To Germany, there with the Emperor
To treat of high affairs touching that time.
Th' advantage of his absence took the King,
And in the meantime sojourn'd at my father's;
Where how he did prevail I shame to speak-
But truth is truth: large lengths of seas and shores
Between my father and my mother lay,
As I have heard my father speak himself,
When this same lusty gentleman was got.
Upon his death-bed he by will bequeath'd
His lands to me, and took it on his death
That this my mother's son was none of his;
And if he were, he came into the world
Full fourteen weeks before the course of time.
Then, good my liege, let me have what is mine,
My father's land, as was my father's will.

oh old Sir Robert, father, I give heaven
thanks upon my knees that I don't look like you!

Why, what a lunatic heaven has sent to us!

He looks rather like the Lionheart;
his voice also sounds like him.
Can't you see some elements of my son
in this man's make up?

I've had a good look over him
and I think he's just like Richard. Speak, sir,
what makes you claim your brother's property?

Because he has a profile like my father.
He thinks that profile should give him all my land:
that imperfect coin wants five hundred pounds a
year!

My good lord, when my father was alive,
your brother often employed my father–

Well, sir, you won't get my land like this:
you must explain how he employed my mother.

And he once sent him as ambassador
to Germany, to discuss important matters
of the time with the Emperor.
The King took advantage of his absence,
staying at my father's place,
and I'm ashamed to say how he succeeded there;
but the truth is the truth: there were great swathes
of land and sea between my father and my mother
when this lively gentleman was conceived–
I've heard my father say that himself.
On his deathbed he left me his lands
in his will, and as he was dying he swore
that my mother's son was not his;
for if he were, he would've had to be born
fourteen weeks ahead of time.
So, my good Lord, let me have what is mine,
my father's land, as my father willed it.

KING JOHN.
Sirrah, your brother is legitimate:
Your father's wife did after wedlock bear him,
And if she did play false, the fault was hers;
Which fault lies on the hazards of all husbands
That marry wives. Tell me, how if my brother,
Who, as you say, took pains to get this son,
Had of your father claim'd this son for his?
In sooth, good friend, your father might have kept
This calf, bred from his cow, from all the world;
In sooth, he might; then, if he were my brother's,
My brother might not claim him; nor your father,
Being none of his, refuse him. This concludes:
My mother's son did get your father's heir;
Your father's heir must have your father's land.

*Sir, your brother's legitimate:
your father's wife had him after they were married,
and if she cheated, that was her sin;
that's a sin all husbands who marry wives
have to risk. Tell me, what if my brother,
whom you claim made great efforts to father this
son, told your father this son was his?
Truly, good friend, your father would have kept
this calf, bred from his cow, hidden from the world;
he really might have; then, if he were my brother's,
my brother might not claim him; and your father,
as it had nothing to do with him, would refuse him.
To conclude:
my mother's son fathered your father's heir,
so your father's heir must have your father's land.*

ROBERT.
Shall then my father's will be of no force
To dispossess that child which is not his?

*So my father's will doesn't have the power
to disinherit the child which isn't his?*

BASTARD.
Of no more force to dispossess me, sir,
Than was his will to get me, as I think.

*He's no more able to disinherit me, sir,
than he was able to conceive me, I think.*

ELINOR.
Whether hadst thou rather be a Faulconbridge,
And like thy brother, to enjoy thy land,
Or the reputed son of Coeur-de-lion,
Lord of thy presence and no land beside?

*Would you rather be a Faulconbridge,
and have the land like your brother,
or be thought of as the son of the Lionheart,
with a lordly title but no land?*

BASTARD.
Madam, an if my brother had my shape
And I had his, Sir Robert's his, like him;
And if my legs were two such riding-rods,
My arms such eel-skins stuff'd, my face so thin
That in mine ear I durst not stick a rose
Lest men should say 'Look where three-farthings goes!'
And, to his shape, were heir to all this land-
Would I might never stir from off this place,
I would give it every foot to have this face!
I would not be Sir Nob in any case.

*Madam, if my brother looked like me,
and I looked like him, like Sir Robert;
if my legs were two beanpoles like his,
my arms like such stuffed eelskins, my face so thin
that I wouldn't dare put a rose behind my ear,
in case men said, "look, there goes a queen!"
If having his body made me heir to the whole country
I would never leave this place,
I would give up every foot of it to keep my own
face! I wouldn't be Sir Robert for anything.*

ELINOR.
I like thee well. Wilt thou forsake thy fortune,
Bequeath thy land to him and follow me?
I am a soldier and now bound to France.

*I like you. Will you give up your fortune,
leave your land to him and follow me?
I am a soldier and am now going to France.*

BASTARD.

Brother, take you my land, I'll take my chance.
Your face hath got five hundred pound a year,
Yet sell your face for fivepence and 'tis dear.
Madam, I'll follow you unto the death.

ELINOR.
Nay, I would have you go before me thither.

BASTARD.
Our country manners give our betters way.

KING JOHN.
What is thy name?

BASTARD.
Philip, my liege, so is my name begun:
Philip, good old Sir Robert's wife's eldest son.

KING JOHN.
From henceforth bear his name whose form thou bearest:
Kneel thou down Philip, but rise more great-
Arise Sir Richard and Plantagenet.

BASTARD.
Brother by th' mother's side, give me your hand;
My father gave me honour, yours gave land.
Now blessed be the hour, by night or day,
When I was got, Sir Robert was away!

ELINOR.
The very spirit of Plantagenet!
I am thy grandam, Richard: call me so.

BASTARD.
Madam, by chance, but not by truth; what though?
Something about, a little from the right,
In at the window, or else o'er the hatch;
Who dares not stir by day must walk by night;
And have is have, however men do catch.
Near or far off, well won is still well shot;
And I am I, howe'er I was begot.

KING JOHN.
Go, Faulconbridge; now hast thou thy desire:
A landless knight makes thee a landed squire.
Come, madam, and come, Richard, we must speed
For France, for France, for it is more than need.

Brother, you take my land, I'll take my chances.
Your face has got you five hundred pounds a year,
but if you sold your face for fivepence that would
be too much. Madam, I'll follow you to the death.

No, if were going there are sooner you were ahead
of me.

In the country we always let our betters go first.

What is your name?

Philip, my lord, is my first name:
Philip, the eldest son of the wife of good old Sir
Robert.

From now on carry the name of the one you
resemble:
kneel down as Philip, but get up greater;
arise Sir Richard and Plantagenet.

Brother or my mother's side, give me your hand;
my father gave me honour, yours gave you land.
May the hour be blessed, whether it was night or
day,
when I was conceived, and Sir Robert was away!

Just like a Plantagenet!
I am your grandmother, Richard: call me that.

Madam, through chance, not honourable conduct;
but so what? Just irregularly, from the side,
in at the window, or else through the hatch;
someone who dares not be seen in the day must
walk in the night; to have is to have, however you
get it. Near or far, if you hit the target it is a good
shot; and I am who I am, however I was conceived.

Go, Faulconbridge; now you have what you want;
a knight without land has made you a landed
gentleman.
Come, madam, and come, Richard, we must hurry
to France, our presence there is essential.

BASTARD.
Brother, adieu. Good fortune come to thee!
For thou wast got i' th' way of honesty.

Exeunt all but the BASTARD

A foot of honour better than I was;
But many a many foot of land the worse.
Well, now can I make any Joan a lady.
'Good den, Sir Richard!'-'God-a-mercy, fellow!'
And if his name be George, I'll call him Peter;
For new-made honour doth forget men's names:
'Tis too respective and too sociable
For your conversion. Now your traveller,
He and his toothpick at my worship's mess-
And when my knightly stomach is suffic'd,
Why then I suck my teeth and catechize
My picked man of countries: 'My dear sir,'
Thus leaning on mine elbow I begin
'I shall beseech you'-That is question now;
And then comes answer like an Absey book:
'O sir,' says answer 'at your best command,
At your employment, at your service, sir!'
'No, sir,' says question 'I, sweet sir, at yours.'
And so, ere answer knows what question would,
Saving in dialogue of compliment,
And talking of the Alps and Apennines,
The Pyrenean and the river Po-
It draws toward supper in conclusion so.
But this is worshipful society,
And fits the mounting spirit like myself;
For he is but a bastard to the time
That doth not smack of observation-
And so am I, whether I smack or no;
And not alone in habit and device,
Exterior form, outward accoutrement,
But from the inward motion to deliver
Sweet, sweet, sweet poison for the age's tooth;
Which, though I will not practise to deceive,
Yet, to avoid deceit, I mean to learn;
For it shall strew the footsteps of my rising.
But who comes in such haste in riding-robes?
What woman-post is this? Hath she no husband
That will take pains to blow a horn before her?

Enter LADY FAULCONBRIDGE, and JAMES GURNEY

O me, 'tis my mother! How now, good lady!

Goodbye, brother: may you have good luck!
For you were conceived legitimately.

[All leave except the Bastard]

I was given a better position,
but lost plenty of land.
Well, now I can make any tart a lady.
"Good day, Sir Richard!"–"God bless you,
fellow!"– And if he is called George, I'll call him
Peter; for newly created noblemen can't remember
men's names: that would be too respectful and too
friendly for your new position. Now a traveller,
sitting with his toothpick at my table, when I've had
plenty to eat, then I shall suck my teeth and
question my chosen travelling man: "my dear sir,"
that's how I'll begin, leaning on my elbow,
"I must ask you,"–that is the question;
and the answer will come back like a textbook:
"Oh sir," says the answer, "I'm yours to command;
I will work for you, I'm at your service, sir."
"No, sir," says the question, "oh I, sweet sir, am at
yours." And so, before he even knows what I want,
except that I want respect,
he'll be talking about the Alps and the Apennines,
the Pyrenees and the River Po,
and so supper comes to an end.
But this is high society,
suitable for someone on the up like me;
I'll only be seen as a bastard by
someone who can't see what I've become;
that which I am, disguised or not.
And not just through my clothes and crest,
the way I look on the outside,
but from the inside I shall provide
sweet flattery for their appetites:
which I won't use to deceive,
but to avoid being deceived, I shall learn about it;
for flattery will be all around me as I rise up.
But who is this coming so quickly in riding clothes?
What female messenger is this? Doesn't she have a
husband to make the effort to blow a horn to show
she's coming?

[Enter Lady Faulconbridge and James Gurney]

Hello! It's my mother.–How are you, good lady?

What brings you here to court so hastily?

LADY FAULCONBRIDGE.
Where is that slave, thy brother?
Where is he
That holds in chase mine honour up and down?

BASTARD.
My brother Robert, old Sir Robert's son?
Colbrand the giant, that same mighty man?
Is it Sir Robert's son that you seek so?

LADY FAULCONBRIDGE.
Sir Robert's son! Ay, thou unreverend boy,
Sir Robert's son! Why scorn'st thou at Sir Robert?
He is Sir Robert's son, and so art thou.

BASTARD.
James Gurney, wilt thou give us leave awhile?

GURNEY.
Good leave, good Philip.

BASTARD.
Philip-Sparrow! James,
There's toys abroad-anon I'll tell thee more.

Exit GURNEY

Madam, I was not old Sir Robert's son;
Sir Robert might have eat his part in me
Upon Good Friday, and ne'er broke his fast.
Sir Robert could do: well-marry, to confess-
Could he get me? Sir Robert could not do it:
We know his handiwork. Therefore, good mother,
To whom am I beholding for these limbs?
Sir Robert never holp to make this leg.

LADY FAULCONBRIDGE.
Hast thou conspired with thy brother too,
That for thine own gain shouldst defend mine honour?
What means this scorn, thou most untoward knave?

BASTARD.
Knight, knight, good mother, Basilisco-like.
What! I am dubb'd; I have it on my shoulder.
But, mother, I am not Sir Robert's son:
I have disclaim'd Sir Robert and my land;

> Why have you come rushing to court?

> Where is that swine, your brother?
> Where is the one who's trying to destroy my honour?

> My brother Robert, the son of old Sir Robert?
> Colbrand the giant, that great man?
> Is it Sir Robert's son that you are looking for?

> Sir Robert's son! Yes, you disrespectful boy,
> Sir Robert's son! Why are you mocking Sir Robert?
> He is Sir Robert's son, and so are you.

> James Gurney, will you give us a moment?

> Certainly, good Philip.

> Philip's a name for sparrows! James,
> gifts have been handed out—I'll tell you more soon.

> Madam, I was not the son of old Sir Robert;
> Sir Robert could have had the part of me he created to eat on Good Friday and not broken his fast. Sir Robert was capable, we might as well admit it, but could he create me? Sir Robert couldn't do it: we know what his children look like. Therefore, good mother, who do I get this body from? Sir Robert never helped to make thisleg.

> Have you conspired with your brother as well, when you ought to be defending my honour? What do you mean by this contempt, you ill mannered scoundrel?

> Knight, knight, good mother, like Basilisco. What! I have been knighted; I've been touched on the shoulder. But mother, I am not the son of Sir Robert: I have given up Sir Robert and my land;

14

Legitimation, name, and all is gone.
Then, good my mother, let me know my father-
Some proper man, I hope. Who was it, mother?

LADY FAULCONBRIDGE.
Hast thou denied thyself a Faulconbridge?

BASTARD.
As faithfully as I deny the devil.

LADY FAULCONBRIDGE.
King Richard Coeur-de-lion was thy father.
By long and vehement suit I was seduc'd
To make room for him in my husband's bed.
Heaven lay not my transgression to my charge!
Thou art the issue of my dear offence,
Which was so strongly urg'd past my defence.

BASTARD.
Now, by this light, were I to get again,
Madam, I would not wish a better father.
Some sins do bear their privilege on earth,
And so doth yours: your fault was not your folly;
Needs must you lay your heart at his dispose,
Subjected tribute to commanding love,
Against whose fury and unmatched force
The aweless lion could not wage the fight
Nor keep his princely heart from Richard's hand.
He that perforce robs lions of their hearts
May easily win a woman's. Ay, my mother,
With all my heart I thank thee for my father!
Who lives and dares but say thou didst not well
When I was got, I'll send his soul to hell.
Come, lady, I will show thee to my kin;
And they shall say when Richard me begot,
If thou hadst said him nay, it had been sin.
Who says it was, he lies; I say 'twas not.

Exeunt

legitimacy, title and everything has gone.
So, my good mother, tell me who my father is—
some good man, I hope. Who was it, mother?

Have you rejected the name of Faulconbridge?

As strongly as I reject the devil.

King Richard the Lionheart was your father.
Through long and aggressive persuasion he seduced me
into making room for him in my husband's bed.
May Heaven not punish me for this sin!
You are the result of my great offence,
which I was almost forced into committing.

Now, I swear, madam, if I was to be
conceived again, I couldn't wish for a better father.
Some sins bring rewards on earth,
and yours does: your sin was not stupid;
you had to give him your heart:
to pay tribute to his commanding love,
whose anger and matchless strength
a courageous lion would not be able to resist,
nor could he defend his princely heart against
Richard's strength. Someone who can rob hearts
from lions can easily win a woman's. Yes, my
mother, I thank you for my father with all my heart!
If there's anyone alive who dares to say that you
did wrong in conceiving me, I'll send his soul to
hell. Come, lady, I will show you to my family;
and they shall say that when Richard conceived me,
it would have been a sin for you to say no to him.
Anyone who says it's a sin is a liar. I say it wasn't.

Act II.

SCENE 1

France. Before Angiers

Enter, on one side, AUSTRIA and forces; on the other, KING PHILIP OF FRANCE, LEWIS the Dauphin, CONSTANCE, ARTHUR, and forces

KING PHILIP.
Before Angiers well met, brave Austria.
Arthur, that great forerunner of thy blood,
Richard, that robb'd the lion of his heart
And fought the holy wars in Palestine,
By this brave duke came early to his grave;
And for amends to his posterity,
At our importance hither is he come
To spread his colours, boy, in thy behalf;
And to rebuke the usurpation
Of thy unnatural uncle, English John.
Embrace him, love him, give him welcome hither.

ARTHUR.
God shall forgive you Coeur-de-lion's death
The rather that you give his offspring life,
Shadowing their right under your wings of war.
I give you welcome with a powerless hand,
But with a heart full of unstained love;
Welcome before the gates of Angiers, Duke.

KING PHILIP.
A noble boy! Who would not do thee right?

AUSTRIA.
Upon thy cheek lay I this zealous kiss
As seal to this indenture of my love:
That to my home I will no more return
Till Angiers and the right thou hast in France,
Together with that pale, that white-fac'd shore,
Whose foot spurns back the ocean's roaring tides
And coops from other lands her islanders-
Even till that England, hedg'd in with the main,
That water-walled bulwark, still secure
And confident from foreign purposes-
Even till that utmost corner of the west
Salute thee for her king. Till then, fair boy,
Will I not think of home, but follow arms.

CONSTANCE.
O, take his mother's thanks, a widow's thanks,
Till your strong hand shall help to give him

Good to meet you here in front of Angiers, brave Austria.
Arthur, your great ancestor,
Richard, who stole the heart from a lion
and fought the holy wars in Palestine,
was brought to an early grave by this brave Duke;
and to make amends he has
come here at our request
to lift his banners, boy, on your behalf;
and to win back the crown stolen
by your unnatural uncle, English John.
Embrace him, love him, and make him welcome.

God will forgive you the death of the Lionheart
because you are giving life to his children,
protecting their rights with your armies.
I welcome you with my hand, which is weak,
but with a heart full of pure love;
welcome here in front of Angiers, Duke.

A noble boy! Who wouldn't support you?

I put this kiss of worship on your cheek
to seal what I contract to do for you out of love:
I shall not return to my home
until Angiers and everything else you have rights to
in France, together with that pale, white cliffed
land, which stands against the roaring tides of the
ocean and protects her islanders against attack
from outside– until that England, surrounded by
the sea, that watery defensive wall, still safe
and secure against foreign attack–
until such time as that far corner of the west
acknowledges you as her king. Until then, sweet
boy, I shall fight, and I shall not think of my home.

Oh, take the thanks of his mother, the thanks of a
widow, until your strong hand has given him the

17

strength
To make a more requital to your love!

AUSTRIA.
The peace of heaven is theirs that lift their swords
In such a just and charitable war.

KING PHILIP.
Well then, to work! Our cannon shall be bent
Against the brows of this resisting town;
Call for our chiefest men of discipline,
To cull the plots of best advantages.
We'll lay before this town our royal bones,
Wade to the market-place in Frenchmen's blood,
But we will make it subject to this boy.

CONSTANCE.
Stay for an answer to your embassy,
Lest unadvis'd you stain your swords with blood;
My Lord Chatillon may from England bring
That right in peace which here we urge in war,
And then we shall repent each drop of blood
That hot rash haste so indirectly shed.

Enter CHATILLON

KING PHILIP.
A wonder, lady! Lo, upon thy wish,
Our messenger Chatillon is arriv'd.
What England says, say briefly, gentle lord;
We coldly pause for thee. Chatillon, speak.

CHATILLON.
Then turn your forces from this paltry siege
And stir them up against a mightier task.
England, impatient of your just demands,
Hath put himself in arms. The adverse winds,
Whose leisure I have stay'd, have given him time
To land his legions all as soon as I;
His marches are expedient to this town,
His forces strong, his soldiers confident.
With him along is come the mother-queen,
An Ate, stirring him to blood and strife;
With her the Lady Blanch of Spain;
With them a bastard of the king's deceas'd;
And all th' unsettled humours of the land-
Rash, inconsiderate, fiery voluntaries,
With ladies' faces and fierce dragons' spleens-
Have sold their fortunes at their native homes,

strength
to be able to give you better thanks for your love!

The reward of those who help to fight in such a justified war is the peace of heaven.

Well then, let's get to work! Our cannon will be aimed at the defences of this resistant town; summon our chief strategists,
so that they can decide the best way to attack. If we have to die in front of this town,
or wade through the blood of Frenchmen to get to the centre, we will make this boy their ruler.

Wait until they answer your message,
to avoid any needless bloodshed;
my Lord Chatillon might bring from England
a message peacefully resigning what we were going to fight for,
and then we shall regret every drop of blood
that we spent so unnecessarily in anger.

A miracle, lady! Look, as you said it,
our messenger Chatillon has come.
Tell us quickly, kind lord, what the English stage; we are holding back our battle for you. Speak, Chatillon.

Then turn your forces away from this insignificant siege and get them ready for a greater task.
England, unsympathetic to your justified requests, has raised an army: the opposing winds,
which kept me waiting, have given him time
to land his armies at the same time as me;
he is marching swiftly towards this town,
his army is strong, his soldiers are confident.
Along with him has come his mother the Queen,
an Ate, urging him onto bloodshed and warfare;
with her is her granddaughter, the Lady Blanche of Spain; with them also is a bastard of the dead king, and all the restless men of the country;
hasty, reckless and fiery volunteers,
with the faces of ladies and the temper of dragons, who have sold their property in their native land,

Bearing their birthrights proudly on their backs,	and are carrying all their possessions on their
To make a hazard of new fortunes here.	backs, to see if they can win a new fortune here:
In brief, a braver choice of dauntless spirits	briefly, there was never such an army of
Than now the English bottoms have waft o'er	brave spirits ever riding across the sea
Did never float upon the swelling tide	to commit crimes and harm in Christendom
To do offence and scathe in Christendom.	as this one the English ships have carried over.
[Drum beats]	
The interruption of their churlish drums	The interruption of their miserable drums
Cuts off more circumstance: they are at hand;	stops me saying more: they are close by,
To parley or to fight, therefore prepare.	to negotiate or to fight; so get ready.

KING PHILIP.

How much unlook'd for is this expedition!	How unexpected this invasion is!

AUSTRIA.

By how much unexpected, by so much	We must match how unexpected it is with our
We must awake endeavour for defence,	efforts to defend ourselves,
For courage mounteth with occasion.	for courage grows as it is needed.
Let them be welcome then; we are prepar'd.	So let's give them a welcome; we are ready.

Enter KING JOHN, ELINOR, BLANCH, the BASTARD, PEMBROKE, and others

KING JOHN.

Peace be to France, if France in peace permit	Peaceful greetings to France, if France will
Our just and lineal entrance to our own!	peacefully allow the justified entrance of we who
If not, bleed France, and peace ascend to heaven,	are claiming our birthright!
Whiles we, God's wrathful agent, do correct	If not, let France bleed and peace go up to heaven,
Their proud contempt that beats His peace to heaven!	while we, the agent of God's anger, punish their arrogant contempt that has sent peace away!

KING PHILIP.

Peace be to England, if that war return	Peaceful greetings to England, if they take back
From France to England, there to live in peace!	their army from France to England, to live
England we love, and for that England's sake	peacefully there. We love England; it is for the
With burden of our armour here we sweat.	sake of England that we are sweating here in our
This toil of ours should be a work of thine;	armour. This work we're doing you should be
But thou from loving England art so far	doing yourselves; but you have so little love for
That thou hast under-wrought his lawful king,	England that you have undermined its lawful King,
Cut off the sequence of posterity,	cut off the rightful succession,
Outfaced infant state, and done a rape	defied the infant majesty, and raped
Upon the maiden virtue of the crown.	the maidenly virtue of the Crown.
Look here upon thy brother Geffrey's face:	You can see your brother Geoffrey's face here;
These eyes, these brows, were moulded out of his;	these eyes, this forehead, were copied from his:
This little abstract doth contain that large	this little sketch contains everything
Which died in Geffrey, and the hand of time	which Geoffrey had: in time it will
Shall draw this brief into as huge a volume.	become a picture as great as him.
That Geffrey was thy elder brother born,	That Geoffrey was born your elder brother,
And this his son; England was Geffrey's right,	and this is his son; England was his by right,
And this is Geffrey's. In the name of God,	and this belongs to Geoffrey; how in the name of

How comes it then that thou art call'd a king,
When living blood doth in these temples beat
Which owe the crown that thou o'er-masterest?

KING JOHN.
From whom hast thou this great commission, France,
To draw my answer from thy articles?

KING PHILIP.
From that supernal judge that stirs good thoughts
In any breast of strong authority
To look into the blots and stains of right.
That judge hath made me guardian to this boy,
Under whose warrant I impeach thy wrong,
And by whose help I mean to chastise it.

KING JOHN.
Alack, thou dost usurp authority.

KING PHILIP.
Excuse it is to beat usurping down.

ELINOR.
Who is it thou dost call usurper, France?

CONSTANCE.
Let me make answer: thy usurping son.

ELINOR.
Out, insolent! Thy bastard shall be king,
That thou mayst be a queen and check the world!

CONSTANCE.
My bed was ever to thy son as true
As thine was to thy husband; and this boy
Liker in feature to his father Geffrey
Than thou and John in manners-being as Eke
As rain to water, or devil to his dam.
My boy a bastard! By my soul, I think
His father never was so true begot;
It cannot be, an if thou wert his mother.

ELINOR.
There's a good mother, boy, that blots thy father.

CONSTANCE.
There's a good grandam, boy, that would blot thee.

---

*God do you come to be called the King,
when living blood still runs through the head
of the one who should be wearing the crown which
you have stolen.*

*Where do you get this great authority, France,
to demand that I answer your accusations?*

*From the celestial judge which inspires good thoughts
in anyone who holds authority, making them
look into injustices.
That judge made me guardian of this boy,
and with his authority I bring charges against you,
and with his help I mean to punish you for them.*

Alas, you are exceeding your authority.

It's justified to revenge a theft.

Who are you calling a thief, France?

Let me answer you: your thieving son.

*Damn you, you insolent woman! You want your
bastard to be King
so that you can be a queen and rule the world!*

*I was always as faithful to your son
as you were to your husband; and this boy
is more like his father in looks
than you and John are in manners—and you are
like rain and water, or the devil and his mother.
My boy a bastard! I swear, even
his father wasn't so faithfully conceived;
he can't have been, if you were his mother.*

That's a good mother, boy, who insults your father.

*That's a good grandmother, boy, who wants to
insult you.*

AUSTRIA.
Peace!

Quiet!

BASTARD.
Hear the crier.

Listen to the bailiff.

AUSTRIA.
What the devil art thou?

Who the devil are you?

BASTARD.
One that will play the devil, sir, with you,
An 'a may catch your hide and you alone.
You are the hare of whom the proverb goes,
Whose valour plucks dead lions by the beard;
I'll smoke your skin-coat an I catch you right;
Sirrah, look to 't; i' faith I will, i' faith.

*Someone who will play the devil with you, sir,
who might have the skin off your back.
You are like the hare in the proverb,
who is so brave that he pulls the beards of dead
lions; I'll give you a good thrashing when I get my
hands on you;
be warned, sir; I swear I will, I swear.*

BLANCH.
O, well did he become that lion's robe
That did disrobe the lion of that robe!

*The one who stole the skin off a lion
would certainly be suited to a lion's skin!*

BASTARD.
It lies as sightly on the back of him
As great Alcides' shows upon an ass;
But, ass, I'll take that burden from your back,
Or lay on that shall make your shoulders crack.

*It looks as good on his back
as the great Alcides looked riding on an ass;
but, ass, I'll take that weight from your back,
or whip you till your shoulders crack.*

AUSTRIA.
What cracker is this same that deafs our ears
With this abundance of superfluous breath?
King Philip, determine what we shall do straight.

*Who is this braggart who is deafening us
with all these wasted words?
King Philip, decide what we shall do at once.*

KING PHILIP.
Women and fools, break off your conference.
King John, this is the very sum of all:
England and Ireland, Anjou, Touraine, Maine,
In right of Arthur, do I claim of thee;
Wilt thou resign them and lay down thy arms?

*Women and fools, stop your chatter.
King John, this is the heart of the matter:
I claim England and Ireland, Anjou, Touraine
and Maine from you as Arthur's rightful property;
will you give them up and put down your weapons?*

KING JOHN.
My life as soon. I do defy thee, France.
Arthur of Britaine, yield thee to my hand,
And out of my dear love I'll give thee more
Than e'er the coward hand of France can win.
Submit thee, boy.

*I would as soon give up my life. I defy you, France.
Arthur of Brittany, surrender to me,
and in my dear love I will give you more
then the cowardly hand of France could ever win
for you. Surrender, boy.*

ELINOR.
Come to thy grandam, child.

Come to your grandmother, child.

CONSTANCE.
Do, child, go to it grandam, child;
Give grandam kingdom, and it grandam will
Give it a plum, a cherry, and a fig.
There's a good grandam!

ARTHUR.
Good my mother, peace!
I would that I were low laid in my grave:
I am not worth this coil that's made for me.

ELINOR.
His mother shames him so, poor boy, he weeps.

CONSTANCE.
Now shame upon you, whe'er she does or no!
His grandam's wrongs, and not his mother's shames,
Draws those heaven-moving pearls from his poor eyes,
Which heaven shall take in nature of a fee;
Ay, with these crystal beads heaven shall be brib'd
To do him justice and revenge on you.

ELINOR.
Thou monstrous slanderer of heaven and earth!

CONSTANCE.
Thou monstrous injurer of heaven and earth,
Call not me slanderer! Thou and thine usurp
The dominations, royalties, and rights,
Of this oppressed boy; this is thy eldest son's son,
Infortunate in nothing but in thee.
Thy sins are visited in this poor child;
The canon of the law is laid on him,
Being but the second generation
Removed from thy sin-conceiving womb.

KING JOHN.
Bedlam, have done.

CONSTANCE.
I have but this to say-
That he is not only plagued for her sin,
But God hath made her sin and her the plague
On this removed issue, plagued for her
And with her plague; her sin his injury,
Her injury the beadle to her sin;
All punish'd in the person of this child,

Go on, child, go to your grandmother, child;
give grandmother a kingdom, and your
grandmother will give you a plum, a cherry, and a
fig. What a good grandmother!

My good mother, quiet!
I wish I was dead in my grave:
I'm not worth the fuss that's being made for me.

He's so ashamed of his mother, poor boy, that he's crying.

The shame is new, whether she does or not!
His grandmother's sins, not the shame of his mother,
is what draws those heavenly tears from his poor eyes,
which heaven shall take as payment;
yes, with those crystal beads heaven will be bribed
to give him justice and take revenge on you.

You monstrous slanderer of heaven and earth!

You monstrous offender of heaven and earth,
do not call me a slanderer! You and yours
overthrow the territories, royalty and rights
of this oppressed boy; this is the son of your eldest son,
and being related to you is his only imperfection.
Your sin is visited on this poor child;
the law of the church demands it,
as he is only two generations
away from your sinful womb.

Madwoman, that's enough.

I've only got this to say—
that not only is he being punished for her sin,
but God has made her sin and her the curse
on this descendant, cursed by her
with her own curse; her sin harms him,
driving on his punishment;
it all falls upon this child,

And all for her-a plague upon her!	and all because of her–a curse on her!

ELINOR.

Thou unadvised scold, I can produce A will that bars the title of thy son.	You ignorant quarreler, I can show you a will that denies the claim of your son.

CONSTANCE.

Ay, who doubts that? A will, a wicked will; A woman's will; a cank'red grandam's will!	Yes, who can doubt that? A will, a wicked will; the will of a woman; the will of a diseased grandmother!

KING PHILIP.

Peace, lady! pause, or be more temperate. It ill beseems this presence to cry aim To these ill-tuned repetitions. Some trumpet summon hither to the walls These men of Angiers; let us hear them speak Whose title they admit, Arthur's or John's.	Quiet, lady! Quiet, or speak more calmly. It's not appropriate for you to repeat these ugly slanders in our presence. Let a trumpet call the men of Angiers to the walls; let's hear them say who they think has the true claim, Arthur or John.

Trumpet sounds. Enter citizens upon the walls

CITIZEN.

Who is it that hath warn'd us to the walls?	Who has summoned us to the walls?

KING PHILIP.

'Tis France, for England.	It's France, in the matter of England.

KING JOHN.

England for itself. You men of Angiers, and my loving subjects-	It's England, for its own business. You men of Angiers, and my loving subjects–

KING PHILIP.

You loving men of Angiers, Arthur's subjects, Our trumpet call'd you to this gentle parle-	You loving men of Angiers, subjects of Arthur, our trumpet called you to this peaceful debate–

KING JOHN.

For our advantage; therefore hear us first. These flags of France, that are advanced here Before the eye and prospect of your town, Have hither march'd to your endamagement; The cannons have their bowels full of wrath, And ready mounted are they to spit forth Their iron indignation 'gainst your walls; All preparation for a bloody siege And merciless proceeding by these French Confront your city's eyes, your winking gates; And but for our approach those sleeping stones That as a waist doth girdle you about By the compulsion of their ordinance By this time from their fixed beds of lime	For our advantage; so listen to us first. These French forces, that have been brought here and placed in front of your town have come here to do you harm. Their cannons are fully loaded and they are ready to hurl their iron anger against your walls; you can see from your closed gates the merciless plans of these French, all ready for a bloody siege; if it wasn't for our arrival these sleeping stones which surround you like a belt would have been smashed to pieces by their artillery,

Had been dishabited, and wide havoc made
For bloody power to rush upon your peace.
But on the sight of us your lawful king,
Who painfully with much expedient march
Have brought a countercheck before your gates,
To save unscratch'd your city's threat'ned cheeks—
Behold, the French amaz'd vouchsafe a parle;
And now, instead of bullets wrapp'd in fire,
To make a shaking fever in your walls,
They shoot but calm words folded up in smoke,
To make a faithless error in your cars;
Which trust accordingly, kind citizens,
And let us in-your King, whose labour'd spirits,
Forwearied in this action of swift speed,
Craves harbourage within your city walls.

KING PHILIP.
When I have said, make answer to us both.
Lo, in this right hand, whose protection
Is most divinely vow'd upon the right
Of him it holds, stands young Plantagenet,
Son to the elder brother of this man,
And king o'er him and all that he enjoys;
For this down-trodden equity we tread
In warlike march these greens before your town,
Being no further enemy to you
Than the constraint of hospitable zeal
In the relief of this oppressed child
Religiously provokes. Be pleased then
To pay that duty which you truly owe
To him that owes it, namely, this young prince;
And then our arms, like to a muzzled bear,
Save in aspect, hath all offence seal'd up;
Our cannons' malice vainly shall be spent
Against th' invulnerable clouds of heaven;
And with a blessed and unvex'd retire,
With unhack'd swords and helmets all unbruis'd,
We will bear home that lusty blood again
Which here we came to spout against your town,
And leave your children, wives, and you, in peace.
But if you fondly pass our proffer'd offer,
'Tis not the roundure of your old-fac'd walls
Can hide you from our messengers of war,
Though all these English and their discipline
Were harbour'd in their rude circumference.
Then tell us, shall your city call us lord
In that behalf which we have challeng'd it;
Or shall we give the signal to our rage,
And stalk in blood to our possession?

a great breach would have been blown
so that their bloody forces could rush in on your
peace. But at the sight of me,
who has through a hard swift march
brought a defence in front of your gates,
to protect you from the threats against your city,
look, the startled French agreed to talk;
and now, instead of fiery bullets
smashing through your walls
they are only shooting quiet deceptive words,
to deceive you and make you make mistakes:
trust them accordingly, kind citizens,
and let me in, your king, whose tired spirits
have been exhausted by our swift march here
and begs for shelter inside your city walls.

When I have spoken then answer us both.
See, on my right hand, that right hand which is
solemnly devoted to protecting the rights of the one
next to him, stands the young Plantagenet,
the son of the elder brother of this man,
king over him and everything he has:
it's because of his stolen rights that we
have marched here with our army onto the fields in
front of your town, we have no other quarrel with
you apart from what we are obliged to do
by God to help this oppressed child. So you should
be happy to do true service to the one who deserves
it, namely this young Prince:
and then our artillery will be like
a muzzled bear, apart from its looks;
the anger of our cannons will harmlessly
be blown into the invulnerable sky;
and with a blessed and unmolested retreat,
with our swords unnotched and our helmets
undamaged, we will take home our lusty blood,
which we were going to spend attacking this town,
and leave your children, your wives and you in
peace.
But if you foolishly reject this offer we are making,
these round ancient stones will not
protect you against our attacks,
even if all these English with their military skills
were sheltering inside them.
So tell us, will your city acknowledge me as lord,
on behalf of the person for whom I demand it?
Or shall I let my rage run free
and take what's mine by spilling blood?

CITIZEN.
In brief: we are the King of England's subjects;
For him, and in his right, we hold this town.

Briefly: we are subjects of the King of England; we hold this town for him, in his name.

KING JOHN.
Acknowledge then the King, and let me in.

Then acknowledge the King, and let me in.

CITIZEN.
That can we not; but he that proves the King,
To him will we prove loyal. Till that time
Have we ramm'd up our gates against the world.

We can't do that; we will only be loyal to someone who proves himself as a king. Until that time we are not letting anyone in.

KING JOHN.
Doth not the crown of England prove the King?
And if not that, I bring you witnesses:
Twice fifteen thousand hearts of England's breed—

Doesn't the Crown of England make me the King? And if it doesn't, I bring you witnesses: thirty thousand hearts bred by England—

BASTARD.
Bastards and else.

Bastards and others.

KING JOHN.
To verify our title with their lives.

To confirm our rights with their lives.

KING PHILIP.
As many and as well-born bloods as those—

There are as many here, and just as well born—

BASTARD.
Some bastards too.

And some bastards as well.

KING PHILIP.
Stand in his face to contradict his claim.

Standing against him to contradict his claim.

CITIZEN.
Till you compound whose right is worthiest,
We for the worthiest hold the right from both.

Until you show who is the most deserving, we will not bow down to either of you.

KING JOHN.
Then God forgive the sin of all those souls
That to their everlasting residence,
Before the dew of evening fall shall fleet
In dreadful trial of our kingdom's king!

Then may God show mercy to all those souls who will be going to their eternal rest before the evening dew falls, in this dreadful battle to see who is king of our kingdom!

KING PHILIP.
Amen, Amen! Mount, chevaliers; to arms!

Amen, amen! Knights, mount; to battle!

BASTARD.
Saint George, that swing'd the dragon, and e'er since
Sits on's horse back at mine hostess' door,

St George, who killed the dragon, and has ever since been sitting on a horse's back outside the pub,

Teach us some fence![To AUSTRIA]Sirrah, were I at home,
At your den, sirrah, with your lioness,
I would set an ox-head to your lion's hide,
And make a monster of you.

AUSTRIA.
Peace! no more.

BASTARD.
O, tremble, for you hear the lion roar!

KING JOHN.
Up higher to the plain, where we'll set forth
In best appoint
ment all our regiments.

BASTARD.
Speed then to take advantage of the field.

KING PHILIP.
It shall be so; and at the other hill
Command the rest to stand. God and our right!

Exeunt

Here, after excursions, enter the HERALD OF FRANCE, with trumpets, to the gates

FRENCH HERALD.
You men of Angiers, open wide your gates
And let young Arthur, Duke of Britaine, in,
Who by the hand of France this day hath made
Much work for tears in many an English mother,
Whose sons lie scattered on the bleeding ground;
Many a widow's husband grovelling lies,
Coldly embracing the discoloured earth;
And victory with little loss doth play
Upon the dancing banners of the French,
Who are at hand, triumphantly displayed,
To enter conquerors, and to proclaim
Arthur of Britaine England's King and yours.

Enter ENGLISH HERALD, with trumpet

ENGLISH HERALD.
Rejoice, you men of Angiers, ring your bells:
King John, your king and England's, doth approach,
Commander of this hot malicious day.

*teach me some fencing![To Austria] Sir, if I was at home,
at your house, sir, with your wife,
I would make a cuckold out of you.*

Peace! That's enough.

Oh, tremble, you can hear the lion roar!

Let's go up higher to the plain, where we will draw up our regiments in the best battle order.

Let's hurry to get the best position.

This shall be so; and on the other hill we will tell the rest to wait. We're fighting for God and our rights!

You men of Angiers, open your gates wide and let young Arthur, Duke of Brittany, in, who through the efforts of the French king has today made many English mothers shed many tears, as their sons are lying scattered on the bloody ground; the husbands of many widows are lying grovelling cold upon the bloody earth; and victory with little damage has lighted upon the dancing banners of the French, who are close by, paraded in triumphant, come to enter as conquerors, and to proclaim Arthur of Brittany as the King of England and of you.

Rejoice, you men of Angiers, ring your bells: King John, King of England and you, is coming, the victor of this bloody battle. The armour in which they marched away so

26

Their armours that march'd hence so silver-bright Hither return all gilt with Frenchmen's blood. There stuck no plume in any English crest That is removed by a staff of France; Our colours do return in those same hands That did display them when we first march'd forth; And like a jolly troop of huntsmen come Our lusty English, all with purpled hands, Dy'd in the dying slaughter of their foes. Open your gates and give the victors way.	shining silver is coming back covered with the blood of Frenchmen. No feather in any English helmet has been removed by any French soldier; our banners are coming back in the same hands who carried them away from here; our lusty Englishmen are coming like a band of jolly huntsmen, with purple hands, dyed with the blood of their enemies. Open your gates and let the victors in.

CITIZEN.

Heralds, from off our tow'rs we might behold From first to last the onset and retire Of both your armies, whose equality By our best eyes cannot be censured. Blood hath bought blood, and blows have answer'd blows; Strength match'd with strength, and power confronted power; Both are alike, and both alike we like. One must prove greatest. While they weigh so even, We hold our town for neither, yet for both.	Heralds, from our towers we could see from beginning to end the attack and retreat of both your armies, and our sharpest eyed men could not see any difference between them. Blood has been paid for with blood, and blows have answered blows; strength was matched with strength, and power attacked power; you are both alike, and we like you both the same. One of you must show yourself as greatest. While you are so evenly matched, our town shall not acknowledge either, while acknowledging both.

Enter the two KINGS, with their powers, at several doors

KING JOHN.

France, hast thou yet more blood to cast away? Say, shall the current of our right run on? Whose passage, vex'd with thy impediment, Shall leave his native channel and o'erswell With course disturb'd even thy confining shores, Unless thou let his silver water keep A peaceful progress to the ocean.	France, have you any more blood to throw away? Tell us, will the stream of our rights keep running? If you keep blocking its passage it will leave its natural course and flood right over your lands, unless you let its silver water carry on its peaceful way to the ocean.

KING PHILIP.

England, thou hast not sav'd one drop of blood In this hot trial more than we of France; Rather, lost more. And by this hand I swear, That sways the earth this climate overlooks, Before we will lay down our just-borne arms, We'll put thee down, 'gainst whom these arms we bear, Or add a royal number to the dead, Gracing the scroll that tells of this war's loss With slaughter coupled to the name of kings.	England, you have not spilled one drop less of blood in this battle than we of France have; in fact, you have lost more. And I swear by this hand, that rules over the earth under the sky, that before we lay down our justified weapons we shall defeat you, whom we carry them against, or add a royal person to the list of dead, gracing the scroll of those who fail in this war by adding the name of Kings to the slaughter.

BASTARD.

Ha, majesty! how high thy glory tow'rs
When the rich blood of kings is set on fire!
O, now doth Death line his dead chaps with steel;
The swords of soldiers are his teeth, his fangs;
And now he feasts, mousing the flesh of men,
In undetermin'd differences of kings.
Why stand these royal fronts amazed thus?
Cry 'havoc!' kings; back to the stained field,
You equal potents, fiery kindled spirits!
Then let confusion of one part confirm
The other's peace. Till then, blows, blood, and death!

Ha, Majesty! How great your glory becomes when the rich blood of kings is stirred up! Now Death has covered his dead cheeks with steel; the soldiers' swords are his teeth, his fangs; and now he is feasting, tearing up the flesh of men, not discriminating between Kings and others. Why are your royal faces looking so confused? Let out the war cry, kings; go back to the bloody field, you equal forces, fiery burning spirits! So let the defeat of one confirm the rule of the other. Until then, let's have blows, blood and death!

KING JOHN.
Whose party do the townsmen yet admit?

Whose side are the townsmen now on?

KING PHILIP.
Speak, citizens, for England; who's your king?

Speak for England, citizens; who is your king?

CITIZEN.
The King of England, when we know the King.

The King of England, when we know who it is.

KING PHILIP.
Know him in us that here hold up his right.

You can see him in me, upholding his rights.

KING JOHN.
In us that are our own great deputy
And bear possession of our person here,
Lord of our presence, Angiers, and of you.

In me who is upholding his own rights and has brought himself here to you, Lord of himself, Angiers, and of you.

CITIZEN.
A greater pow'r than we denies all this;
And till it be undoubted, we do lock
Our former scruple in our strong-barr'd gates;
King'd of our fears, until our fears, resolv'd,
Be by some certain king purg'd and depos'd.

A greater power than us denies all this; until the question is settled, we shall keep our doubts behind our strongly barred gates; we shall be ruled by our fears until they are removed, overthrown by some true king.

BASTARD.
By heaven, these scroyles of Angiers flout you, kings,
And stand securely on their battlements
As in a theatre, whence they gape and point
At your industrious scenes and acts of death.
Your royal presences be rul'd by me:
Do like the mutines of Jerusalem,
Be friends awhile, and both conjointly bend
Your sharpest deeds of malice on this town.
By east and west let France and England mount
Their battering cannon, charged to the mouths,

By heaven, these scoundrels of Angiers are mocking you, Kings, standing as safely on their battlements as they would in a theatre, from where they gape and point at all your hard work and your deaths. Let your royal persons be ruled by me: be like the mutineers in Jerusalem, become allies for a while and both together launch your hardest attacks against this town. Let France and England from the East and West aim their battering cannon, fully charged,

Till their soul-fearing clamours have brawl'd down The flinty ribs of this contemptuous city. I'd play incessantly upon these jades, Even till unfenced desolation Leave them as naked as the vulgar air. That done, dissever your united strengths And part your mingled colours once again, Turn face to face and bloody point to point; Then in a moment Fortune shall cull forth Out of one side her happy minion, To whom in favour she shall give the day, And kiss him with a glorious victory. How like you this wild counsel, mighty states? Smacks it not something of the policy?	*until their terrifying rage has smashed down the stone walls of this arrogant city: I would smash away at these poor creatures until they are left exposed to the open air, with no protection. Once you've done that, untangle your forces, and separate your joint flags once again; face each other again, bloody point to point; then, in that instant, Fortune will choose whom she favours out of the two sides, and she shall allow him to triumph, and reward him with a glorious victory. What do you think of this daring advice, great Kings? Don't you think it sounds cunning?*

KING JOHN.
Now, by the sky that hangs above our heads,
I like it well. France, shall we knit our pow'rs
And lay this Angiers even with the ground;
Then after fight who shall be king of it?

Now, I swear by the heavens above, I like it. France, shall we join forces to raze this Angiers to the ground, and then afterwards fight for who shall be king of it?

BASTARD.
An if thou hast the mettle of a king,
Being wrong'd as we are by this peevish town,
Turn thou the mouth of thy artillery,
As we will ours, against these saucy walls;
And when that we have dash'd them to the ground,
Why then defy each other, and pell-mell
Make work upon ourselves, for heaven or hell.

If you have the spirit of the King, having been insulted as we have been by this petulant town, turn the muzzles of your artillery, as we will, against their cheeky walls; and when we have smashed them to the ground, well then we will fight each other, and chaotically attack ourselves, for better or for worse.

KING PHILIP.
Let it be so. Say, where will you assault?

I agree. Tell me where you will attack?

KING JOHN.
We from the west will send destruction
Into this city's bosom.

I shall send my forces into the heart of the city from the West.

AUSTRIA.
I from the north.

I shall attack from the North.

KING PHILIP.
Our thunder from the south
Shall rain their drift of bullets on this town.

We shall rain a storm of bullets on this town from the South.

BASTARD.
[Aside] O prudent discipline! From north to south,
Austria and France shoot in each other's mouth.
I'll stir them to it.–Come, away, away!

A clever plan! From North to South Austria and France will be shooting at each other. I'll encourage them to do it.–Come, let's go, let's go!

29

CITIZEN.
Hear us, great kings: vouchsafe awhile to stay,
And I shall show you peace and fair-fac'd league;
Win you this city without stroke or wound;
Rescue those breathing lives to die in beds
That here come sacrifices for the field.
Persever not, but hear me, mighty kings.

KING JOHN.
Speak on with favour; we are bent to hear.

CITIZEN.
That daughter there of Spain, the Lady Blanch,
Is niece to England; look upon the years
Of Lewis the Dauphin and that lovely maid.
If lusty love should go in quest of beauty,
Where should he find it fairer than in Blanch?
If zealous love should go in search of virtue,
Where should he find it purer than in Blanch?
If love ambitious sought a match of birth,
Whose veins bound richer blood than Lady Blanch?
Such as she is, in beauty, virtue, birth,
Is the young Dauphin every way complete-
If not complete of, say he is not she;
And she again wants nothing, to name want,
If want it be not that she is not he.
He is the half part of a blessed man,
Left to be finished by such as she;
And she a fair divided excellence,
Whose fulness of perfection lies in him.
O, two such silver currents, when they join,
Do glorify the banks that bound them in;
And two such shores to two such streams made one,
Two such controlling bounds, shall you be, Kings,
To these two princes, if you marry them.
This union shall do more than battery can
To our fast-closed gates; for at this match
With swifter spleen than powder can enforce,
The mouth of passage shall we fling wide ope
And give you entrance; but without this match,
The sea enraged is not half so deaf,
Lions more confident, mountains and rocks
More free from motion-no, not Death himself
In mortal fury half so peremptory
As we to keep this city.

BASTARD.

Hear us, great Kings: agree to wait a while,
and I will show you peace and sweet agreement;
you can win this city without any losses;
you can let those who have come here to sacrifice themselves
on the battlefield die in their beds.
Do not carry on, but listen to me, mighty kings.

You may keep talking; we are listening.

That daughter of Spain there, the Lady Blanche,
is close to King John: look at the age
of the Dauphin Louis and that lovely girl:
if a strong young love should go in search of
beauty, where would he find it better than in her?
If pious love goes in search of goodness,
where would he find it more pure than in Blanche?
If ambitious love sought a good match,
who has nobler blood in their veins than Lady Blanche?
Everything she is, in beauty, goodness and nobility,
is matched by the young Dauphin:
if he doesn't match it, say he is not her,
and if she is lacking anything he has
then you can say that she is not him:
he is half a part of a blessed man,
waiting to be completed by someone like her;
and she is half of an excellent woman,
who can be completed by him.
Two such silver streams, when they join,
make the country they run through glorious;
and with two such shores, two such streams running into one,
you will be two controlling banks to them, kings,
if you join them together in marriage.
This marriage would be more likely to open our
solidly closed gates than any artillery; if it
happened we would fling our gates wide open
faster than any assault could hope to do,
and let you in: but without the marriage
the raging sea is not half as deaf,
lions not half as confident, mountains and rocks
more still, no, death himself
is not so determined as he seeks out mortals
as we will be in defending our city.

Here's a stay
That shakes the rotten carcass of old Death
Out of his rags! Here's a large mouth, indeed,
That spits forth death and mountains, rocks and seas;
Talks as familiarly of roaring lions
As maids of thirteen do of puppy-dogs!
What cannoneer begot this lusty blood?
He speaks plain cannon-fire, and smoke and bounce;
He gives the bastinado with his tongue;
Our ears are cudgell'd; not a word of his
But buffets better than a fist of France.
Zounds! I was never so bethump'd with words
Since I first call'd my brother's father dad.

ELINOR.
Son, list to this conjunction, make this match;
Give with our niece a dowry large enough;
For by this knot thou shalt so surely tie
Thy now unsur'd assurance to the crown
That yon green boy shall have no sun to ripe
The bloom that promiseth a mighty fruit.
I see a yielding in the looks of France;
Mark how they whisper. Urge them while their souls
Are capable of this ambition,
Lest zeal, now melted by the windy breath
Of soft petitions, pity, and remorse,
Cool and congeal again to what it was.

CITIZEN.
Why answer not the double majesties
This friendly treaty of our threat'ned town?

KING PHILIP.
Speak England first, that hath been forward first
To speak unto this city: what say you?

KING JOHN.
If that the Dauphin there, thy princely son,
Can in this book of beauty read 'I love,'
Her dowry shall weigh equal with a queen;
For Anjou, and fair Touraine, Maine, Poictiers,
And all that we upon this side the sea-
Except this city now by us besieg'd-
Find liable to our crown and dignity,
Shall gild her bridal bed, and make her rich
In titles, honours, and promotions,

*Here's an obstacle
that will shake the rotten carcass of old Death
out of his rags! Here's a brave talker,
who goes on about death and mountains, rocks and seas;
talks as casually about roaring lions
as girls of thirteen do about puppies!
What artillery man fathered this lusty chap?
He speaks like a cannon, with smoke and explosions;
his tongue is like a club,
it cudgels our ears; everything he says
makes a better attack than any blows of France.
By God! I was never so clobbered with words
since I first called my brother's father dad.*

*Son, listen to this scheme, make this marriage;
give a good large dowry with our niece;
for making this marriage you will make your
currently dubious claim to the crown so solid
that that young lad will have no chance
of developing his claim.
I can see doubt in the looks of the French;
look how they whisper. Encourage them while they are
keen on this plan,
in case their keenness, strong at the moment due to
soft petitions, pity and remorse,
cools down again and returns to how it was.*

*Why do the two kings not answer
this friendly request by our threatened town?*

*Let England speak first, who was the first one
to speak to this city: what do you say?*

*If your princely son, that Dauphin there,
looks at this beauty and loves her,
she shall have a dowry equal to the Queen;
Anjou, fair Touraine, Maine, Poitiers,
and everything that is ours on this side of the
Channel– except for this city we are now
besieging– that is subject to our rule,
will decorate her bridal bed, and make her rich
in titles, honours and promotions,*

As she in beauty, education, blood,
Holds hand with any princess of the world.

KING PHILIP.
What say'st thou, boy? Look in the lady's face.

LEWIS.
I do, my lord, and in her eye I find
A wonder, or a wondrous miracle,
The shadow of myself form'd in her eye;
Which, being but the shadow of your son,
Becomes a sun, and makes your son a shadow.
I do protest I never lov'd myself
Till now infixed I beheld myself
Drawn in the flattering table of her eye.

[Whispers with BLANCH]

BASTARD.
[Aside] Drawn in the flattering table of her eye,
Hang'd in the frowning wrinkle of her brow,
And quarter'd in her heart-he doth espy
Himself love's traitor. This is pity now,
That hang'd and drawn and quarter'd there should be
In such a love so vile a lout as he.

BLANCH.
My uncle's will in this respect is mine.
If he see aught in you that makes him like,
That anything he sees which moves his liking
I can with ease translate it to my will;
Or if you will, to speak more properly,
I will enforce it eas'ly to my love.
Further I will not flatter you, my lord,
That all I see in you is worthy love,
Than this: that nothing do I see in you-
Though churlish thoughts themselves should be your judge-
That I can find should merit any hate.

KING JOHN.
What say these young ones? What say you, my niece?

BLANCH.
That she is bound in honour still to do
What you in wisdom still vouchsafe to say.

---

as rich as she is in beauty, education and nobility, so that she can match any princess in the world.

What do you say, boy? Look at the lady's face.

I am, my lord, and in her eyes I see something amazing, perhaps a miracle, the shape of myself formed in her eye; which, being only the shadow of your son, becomes a sun, and makes your son a shadow. I must say that I never loved myself until now when I see myself drawn in the flattering mirror of her eyes.

Drawn in the flattering mirror of her eyes, hanged on the frowning wrinkles of her forehead, and quartered in her heart—he sees himself as a traitor to love. It's a pity now that such a vile lout as him should be hung drawn and quartered there.

What my uncle wishes in this matter is what I wish. If he sees anything in you that he likes, if there is anything about you which makes him like you, I can certainly make that liking my own; or if you wish, to be more accurate, I can easily make it part of my love. I will not flatter you any further, my lord, other than to say that all I see in you is worthy love: but I don't see anything in you— even judging by the harshest standards— that gives me any reason to hate you.

What do these young ones say? What do you say, my niece?

That I am honour bound to do whatever you wisely decide I should.

KING JOHN.
Speak then, Prince Dauphin; can you love this lady?

LEWIS.
Nay, ask me if I can refrain from love;
For I do love her most unfeignedly.

KING JOHN.
Then do I give Volquessen, Touraine, Maine,
Poictiers, and Anjou, these five provinces,
With her to thee; and this addition more,
Full thirty thousand marks of English coin.
Philip of France, if thou be pleas'd withal,
Command thy son and daughter to join hands.

KING PHILIP.
It likes us well; young princes, close your hands.

AUSTRIA.
And your lips too; for I am well assur'd
That I did so when I was first assur'd.

KING PHILIP.
Now, citizens of Angiers, ope your gates,
Let in that amity which you have made;
For at Saint Mary's chapel presently
The rites of marriage shall be solemniz'd.
Is not the Lady Constance in this troop?
I know she is not; for this match made up
Her presence would have interrupted much.
Where is she and her son? Tell me, who knows.

LEWIS.
She is sad and passionate at your Highness' tent.

KING PHILIP.
And, by my faith, this league that we have made
Will give her sadness very little cure.
Brother of England, how may we content
This widow lady? In her right we came;
Which we, God knows, have turn'd another way,
To our own vantage.

KING JOHN.
We will heal up all,
For we'll create young Arthur Duke of Britaine,
And Earl of Richmond; and this rich fair town
We make him lord of. Call the Lady Constance;

You speak then, Prince Dauphin; can you love this lady?

No, ask me if I can stop myself loving her; for I love her without trying.

Then I shall give Volquessen, Touraine, Maine, Poitiers and Anjou, these five provinces, to you along with her; and I shall also add thirty thousand marks in English money. Philip of France, if you agree to all that, tell your son and daughter to join hands.

I'm very pleased with it; young Princes, hold hands.

And touch lips too; I can certainly remember that I did so when I was first engaged.

*Now, citizens of Angiers, open your gates, and let in the love which you have created; we shall celebrate the marriage at once in St Mary's Chapel.
Isn't Lady Constance in this gathering? I know she is not; for she would have done her best to interrupt this marriage.
Where are her and her son? If anyone knows, tell me.*

She is at your Highness' tent, deeply sad.

*And, I swear, this agreement we have made will not make her any happier.
Brother of England, how can we make this widow happy? We came here to fight for her; but now, God knows, we have changed direction, for our own good.*

We will heal everything, for we will make young Arthur Duke of Brittany, and Earl of Richmond; and also Lord of this rich fair town. Call Lady Constance;

33

Some speedy messenger bid her repair
To our solemnity. I trust we shall,
If not fill up the measure of her will,
Yet in some measure satisfy her so
That we shall stop her exclamation.
Go we as well as haste will suffer us
To this unlook'd-for, unprepared pomp.

Exeunt all but the BASTARD

BASTARD.
Mad world! mad kings! mad composition!
John, to stop Arthur's tide in the whole,
Hath willingly departed with a part;
And France, whose armour conscience buckled on,
Whom zeal and charity brought to the field
As God's own soldier, rounded in the ear
With that same purpose-changer, that sly devil,
That broker that still breaks the pate of faith,
That daily break-vow, he that wins of all,
Of kings, of beggars, old men, young men, maids,
Who having no external thing to lose
But the word 'maid,' cheats the poor maid of that;
That smooth-fac'd gentleman, tickling commodity,
Commodity, the bias of the world-
The world, who of itself is peised well,
Made to run even upon even ground,
Till this advantage, this vile-drawing bias,
This sway of motion, this commodity,
Makes it take head from all indifferency,
From all direction, purpose, course, intent-
And this same bias, this commodity,
This bawd, this broker, this all-changing word,
Clapp'd on the outward eye of fickle France,
Hath drawn him from his own determin'd aid,
From a resolv'd and honourable war,
To a most base and vile-concluded peace.
And why rail I on this commodity?
But for because he hath not woo'd me yet;
Not that I have the power to clutch my hand
When his fair angels would salute my palm,
But for my hand, as unattempted yet,
Like a poor beggar raileth on the rich.
Well, whiles I am a beggar, I will rail
And say there is no sin but to be rich;
And being rich, my virtue then shall be
To say there is no vice but beggary.
Since kings break faith upon commodity,
Gain, be my lord, for I will worship thee.

*let some speedy messenger summon her
to our presence. I hope we shall,
if we can't do everything she wants,
at least we can give her enough satisfaction
so we can stop her complaining.
Let's go as quickly as we can
to this unexpected, unprepared ceremony.*

*Mad world! Mad kings! A mad arrangement!
John, to stop Arthur getting the whole thing
has willingly given up part of it:
and France, who was driven by conscience,
he came to the battlefield in pious charity
as a soldier of God, listened to the whispers
of that sly devil who makes men changeable,
that pimp who destroys all faith,
the daily promise breaker, who wins over everyone,
Kings, beggars, old men, young men, maids,
who, having nothing outside to lose
apart from the word "maid" cheats the poor maid
out of that, that deceitful gentleman, flattering self-
interest, self-interest, which unbalances the world,
the world, which is well-balanced in itself,
designed to run evenly along even ground,
until this bias comes in,
this changing motion, this self-interest,
which makes it run away from impartiality,
from all sense, purpose, and intentions:
this same bias, this self-interest,
this pimp, this broker, this always changing word,
has suddenly popped up in the eyes of fickle
France, and drawn him away from his own
determined path, from a settled and honourable
war to a dishonourable tawdry peace.
Why am I criticising this self-interest?
Because it hasn't come to offer me anything yet;
I don't have the power within my hands
which would make it worth his while;
and so my hand, yet to be tempted,
criticises the rich like a poor beggar.
Well, while I am a beggar, I will criticise
and say the only sin is to be rich;
once I'm rich, I shall then say that the only evil
thing is begging. Since kings break their promises
out of self-interest,
gain, be my Lord, for I will worship you!*

Exit

Act III

SCENE 1.

France. The FRENCH KING'S camp

Enter CONSTANCE, ARTHUR, and SALISBURY

CONSTANCE.
Gone to be married! Gone to swear a peace!
False blood to false blood join'd! Gone to be friends!
Shall Lewis have Blanch, and Blanch those provinces?
It is not so; thou hast misspoke, misheard;
Be well advis'd, tell o'er thy tale again.
It cannot be; thou dost but say 'tis so;
I trust I may not trust thee, for thy word
Is but the vain breath of a common man:
Believe me I do not believe thee, man;
I have a king's oath to the contrary.
Thou shalt be punish'd for thus frighting me,
For I am sick and capable of fears,
Oppress'd with wrongs, and therefore full of fears;
A widow, husbandless, subject to fears;
A woman, naturally born to fears;
And though thou now confess thou didst but jest,
With my vex'd spirits I cannot take a truce,
But they will quake and tremble all this day.
What dost thou mean by shaking of thy head?
Why dost thou look so sadly on my son?
What means that hand upon that breast of thine?
Why holds thine eye that lamentable rheum,
Like a proud river peering o'er his bounds?
Be these sad signs confirmers of thy words?
Then speak again-not all thy former tale,
But this one word, whether thy tale be true.

SALISBURY.
As true as I believe you think them false
That give you cause to prove my saying true.

CONSTANCE.
O, if thou teach me to believe this sorrow,
Teach thou this sorrow how to make me die;
And let belief and life encounter so
As doth the fury of two desperate men
Which in the very meeting fall and die!
Lewis marry Blanch! O boy, then where art thou?
France friend with England; what becomes of me?
Fellow, be gone: I cannot brook thy sight;

Gone to be married! Gone to swear to a peace agreement! Joining false blood with false blood! Gone to be friends!
Will Louis have Blanche, and Blanche have these provinces?
It isn't true; you've described it wrong, or misheard; think about it, tell your story over again.
It cannot be; it's just that you say it's true.
I'm sure I can't trust you, for your words are just the useless breath of a common man; believe me, I do not believe you, man: the King has sworn differently to me.
You shall be punished for frightening me like this, for I am sick and liable to take fright, crushed down by insults and so liable to take fright, a widow, husbandless, so liable to take fright, a woman, so naturally liable to take fright; and even if you now admit that you were just joking I will not be able to calm my troubled spirits, but I will shake and tremble the whole day long.
What do you mean by shaking your head like that?
Why are you looking at my son with such sadness?
Why are you holding your hand on your chest?
Why are your eyes full of sad tears, like a proud river about to flood?
Are these sad signs confirmation of what you say?
Then speak again; not everything you just said, but in a word, whether you're telling the truth.

I think my words are as true as you believe them to be false,
and that should tell you that what I've said is true.

Oh, if you persuade me to believe this sadness, then tell this sorrow to kill me; let my belief in it and my life come together like two desperate fighting men who kill each other when they meet!
Louis married Blanche! Oh boy, where does that leave you? France friends with England; what will happen to me? Fellow, get out: I can't stand to look at you;

37

This news hath made thee a most ugly man. | this news has made you a very ugly man.

SALISBURY.
What other harm have I, good lady, done
But spoke the harm that is by others done?

| What harm have I done good lady, apart from telling you the bad things that others have done?

CONSTANCE.
Which harm within itself so heinous is
As it makes harmful all that speak of it.

| Those bad things are so bad that anyone who speaks of them becomes bad also.

ARTHUR.
I do beseech you, madam, be content.

| Please, madam, calm yourself.

CONSTANCE.
If thou that bid'st me be content wert grim,
Ugly, and sland'rous to thy mother's womb,
Full of unpleasing blots and sightless stains,
Lame, foolish, crooked, swart, prodigious,
Patch'd with foul moles and eye-offending marks,
I would not care, I then would be content;
For then I should not love thee; no, nor thou
Become thy great birth, nor deserve a crown.
But thou art fair, and at thy birth, dear boy,
Nature and Fortune join'd to make thee great:
Of Nature's gifts thou mayst with lilies boast,
And with the half-blown rose; but Fortune, O!
She is corrupted, chang'd, and won from thee;
Sh' adulterates hourly with thine uncle John,
And with her golden hand hath pluck'd on France
To tread down fair respect of sovereignty,
And made his majesty the bawd to theirs.
France is a bawd to Fortune and King John-
That strumpet Fortune, that usurping John!
Tell me, thou fellow, is not France forsworn?
Envenom him with words, or get thee gone
And leave those woes alone which I alone
Am bound to under-bear.

| If you, who tells me to be calm, were horrid, ugly, an insult to your mother's womb, covered with revolting patches and unsightly stains, lame, foolish, crooked, swarthy, deformed, covered with foul moles and offensive marks, I wouldn't care, I would be happy, for then I wouldn't love you: no, and you wouldn't be suited to your noble birth, nor would you deserve a crown. But you are handsome, and when you were born, dear boy, nature and fortune joined together to make you great: nature has made you comparable to the lilies and a half blossomed rose. But fortune, oh, she has been corrupted, changed and taken away from you; she is unfaithful to you with your uncle John, and has with her golden hand chosen France to ride roughshod over the fair respect due to sovereignty, and made his majesty a pimp to theirs. France is a pimp to fortune and King John, that harlot fortune, that theiving John! Tell me, fellow, has France broken his oath? Curse him to me, or get out, and leave me alone with those sorrows which I am going to have to endure alone!

SALISBURY.
Pardon me, madam,
I may not go without you to the kings.

| I'm sorry, madam, I can't go back to the kings without you.

CONSTANCE.
Thou mayst, thou shalt; I will not go with thee;
I will instruct my sorrows to be proud,
For grief is proud, and makes his owner stoop.
To me, and to the state of my great grief,
Let kings assemble; for my grief's so great
That no supporter but the huge firm earth

| You can, and you will; I won't go with you; I will tell my sorrows to be proud, for grief is proud, and bows down his owner. Let the kings come here to me and see my great grief; it's so great that only the huge firm earth

Can hold it up.
[Seats herself on the ground]
Here I and sorrows sit;
Here is my throne, bid kings come bow to it.

is strong enough to support it.
This is where I will sit with my sorrows;
this is my throne, tell the kings to come and bow to it.

Enter KING JOHN, KING PHILIP, LEWIS, BLANCH, ELINOR, the BASTARD, AUSTRIA, and attendants

KING PHILIP.
'Tis true, fair daughter, and this blessed day
Ever in France shall be kept festival.
To solemnize this day the glorious sun
Stays in his course and plays the alchemist,
Turning with splendour of his precious eye
The meagre cloddy earth to glittering gold.
The yearly course that brings this day about
Shall never see it but a holiday.

It's true, fair daughter, and this blessed day
will always be a holiday in France from now on.
To celebrate this day the glorious sun
has stopped on his journey and is playing the alchemist,
using the splendour of his precious light
to turn the dull clods into glittering gold.
Every year when this day comes around
it will always be a holiday.

CONSTANCE.
[Rising] A wicked day, and not a holy day!
What hath this day deserv'd? what hath it done
That it in golden letters should be set
Among the high tides in the calendar?
Nay, rather turn this day out of the week,
This day of shame, oppression, perjury;
Or, if it must stand still, let wives with child
Pray that their burdens may not fall this day,
Lest that their hopes prodigiously be cross'd;
But on this day let seamen fear no wreck;
No bargains break that are not this day made;
This day, all things begun come to ill end,
Yea, faith itself to hollow falsehood change!

A wicked day, and not a holy day!
What's so good about this day? What happened on
it that it should be given golden letters and placed
amongst the Festival days in the calendar?
No, you should throw this day out of the week,
this day of shame, oppression and perjury;
or, if it has to stay, let pregnant wives
pray that their children will not be born on this
day, in case they turn out to be horribly unlucky;
let sailors fear this day as the worst for wrecks;
break any bargains that are made on it;
everything done on this day will come to a bad end,
why, faith itself will change to hollow falsehood!

KING PHILIP.
By heaven, lady, you shall have no cause
To curse the fair proceedings of this day.
Have I not pawn'd to you my majesty?

By heaven, lady, you shall have no reason
to curse the fair events of this day.
Haven't I loaned you my majesty?

CONSTANCE.
You have beguil'd me with a counterfeit
Resembling majesty, which, being touch'd and tried,
Proves valueless; you are forsworn, forsworn;
You came in arms to spill mine enemies' blood,
But now in arms you strengthen it with yours.
The grappling vigour and rough frown of war
Is cold in amity and painted peace,
And our oppression hath made up this league.
Arm, arm, you heavens, against these perjur'd

You have tricked me with a forgery
resembling Majesty, which, being touched and tested,
proves to be valueless; you have broken your oath;
you came armed to spill blood of my enemies,
but now, armed, you are strengthening his blood
with yours. The fighting strength and rough frown
of war has become cold in friendship and patched
up peace, and this agreement is sealed by the
wrongs you have done us. Take arms, you heavens,

kings!
A widow cries: Be husband to me, heavens!
Let not the hours of this ungodly day
Wear out the day in peace; but, ere sunset,
Set armed discord 'twixt these perjur'd kings!
Hear me, O, hear me!

AUSTRIA.
Lady Constance, peace!

CONSTANCE.
War! war! no peace! Peace is to me a war.
O Lymoges! O Austria! thou dost shame
That bloody spoil. Thou slave, thou wretch, thou coward!
Thou little valiant, great in villainy!
Thou ever strong upon the stronger side!
Thou Fortune's champion that dost never fight
But when her humorous ladyship is by
To teach thee safety! Thou art perjur'd too,
And sooth'st up greatness. What a fool art thou,
A ramping fool, to brag and stamp and swear
Upon my party! Thou cold-blooded slave,
Hast thou not spoke like thunder on my side,
Been sworn my soldier, bidding me depend
Upon thy stars, thy fortune, and thy strength,
And dost thou now fall over to my foes?
Thou wear a lion's hide! Doff it for shame,
And hang a calf's-skin on those recreant limbs.

AUSTRIA.
O that a man should speak those words to me!

BASTARD.
And hang a calf's-skin on those recreant limbs.

AUSTRIA.
Thou dar'st not say so, villain, for thy life.

BASTARD.
And hang a calf's-skin on those recreant limbs.

KING JOHN.
We like not this: thou dost forget thyself.

Enter PANDULPH

KING PHILIP.
Here comes the holy legate of the Pope.

PANDULPH.
Hail, you anointed deputies of heaven!
To thee, King John, my holy errand is.
I Pandulph, of fair Milan cardinal,
And from Pope Innocent the legate here,
Do in his name religiously demand
Why thou against the Church, our holy mother,
So wilfully dost spurn; and force perforce
Keep Stephen Langton, chosen Archbishop
Of Canterbury, from that holy see?
This, in our foresaid holy father's name,
Pope Innocent, I do demand of thee.

KING JOHN.
What earthly name to interrogatories
Can task the free breath of a sacred king?
Thou canst not, Cardinal, devise a name
So slight, unworthy, and ridiculous,
To charge me to an answer, as the Pope.
Tell him this tale, and from the mouth of England
Add thus much more, that no Italian priest
Shall tithe or toll in our dominions;
But as we under heaven are supreme head,
So, under Him that great supremacy,
Where we do reign we will alone uphold,
Without th' assistance of a mortal hand.
So tell the Pope, all reverence set apart
To him and his usurp'd authority.

KING PHILIP.
Brother of England, you blaspheme in this.

KING JOHN.
Though you and all the kings of Christendom
Are led so grossly by this meddling priest,
Dreading the curse that money may buy out,
And by the merit of vile gold, dross, dust,
Purchase corrupted pardon of a man,
Who in that sale sells pardon from himself-
Though you and all the rest, so grossly led,
This juggling witchcraft with revenue cherish;
Yet I alone, alone do me oppose
Against the Pope, and count his friends my foes.

PANDULPH.
Then by the lawful power that I have
Thou shalt stand curs'd and excommunicate;
And blessed shall he be that doth revolt

Greetings, you chosen representatives of heaven!
My holy errand is to you, King John.
I, Pandulph, cardinal of fair Milan,
and the representative of Pope Innocent here,
to religiously demand in his name to know
why you are wilfully disobeying the orders of
the church, our holy mother; why are you using
force to keep Stephen Langton, chosen Archbishop
of Canterbury, from his holy office?
I ask you the question in the name of
our aforementioned holy father, Pope Innocent.

What earthly man has a right to demand answers
from a free and sacred king?
You couldn't invent a name, Cardinal,
so insignificant, unworthy and silly
to demand an answer from me, as the Pope.
Tell him this, and from the mouth of England's
King add this as well, that no Italian priest
will be allowed to raise taxes or tolls in my
kingdom; as I am the supreme ruler on earth,
so, under the guidance of the supreme God,
where I rule I will rule alone,
without the assistance of a mortal man.
Tell the Pope this, that there is no respect
for him or his stolen power.

Brother of England, this is blasphemy.

Although you and all the kings of Christendom
are led so disgracefully by this meddling priest,
dreading the curse that you can bribe your way out
of, and by using vile gold, dross, dust,
you can buy a corrupted pardon from a man
who in the selling sells his own right to a pardon—
though you and all the rest are so disgracefully led,
supporting this juggling witchcraft with funds;
I set myself alone to oppose
the Pope, and I regard his friends as my enemies.

Then by the power invested in me
I say you are cursed and excommunicated;
anyone who revolts against his allegiance

From his allegiance to an heretic; And meritorious shall that hand be call'd, Canonized, and worshipp'd as a saint, That takes away by any secret course Thy hateful life.	to a heretic shall be blessed; and anyone who takes away your revolting life by any means at all shall be called a deserving man and shall be canonised and worshipped as a saint.
CONSTANCE. O, lawful let it be That I have room with Rome to curse awhile! Good father Cardinal, cry thou 'amen' To my keen curses; for without my wrong There is no tongue hath power to curse him right.	Oh, let it be legal for me to join in with Rome in this cursing! Good father Cardinal, cry out "amen" to my sharp curses; for without my wrongs your tongue does not have the power to curse him rightly.
PANDULPH. There's law and warrant, lady, for my curse.	I have legal justification and permission, lady, for my curse.
CONSTANCE. And for mine too; when law can do no right, Let it be lawful that law bar no wrong; Law cannot give my child his kingdom here, For he that holds his kingdom holds the law; Therefore, since law itself is perfect wrong, How can the law forbid my tongue to curse?	And for mine too; when the law cannot do right, let it be lawful for it not to bar any wrong; law cannot give my child his kingdom here, because the one who rules the kingdom makes the laws; so, since the law itself is completely wrong, how can the law ban me from cursing?
PANDULPH. Philip of France, on peril of a curse, Let go the hand of that arch-heretic, And raise the power of France upon his head, Unless he do submit himself to Rome.	Philip of France, unless you want to be cursed, release the hand of that arch heretic, and attack him with the forces of France, unless he bows down to Rome.
ELINOR. Look'st thou pale, France? Do not let go thy hand.	Why are you looking pale, France? Don't release his hand.
CONSTANCE. Look to that, devil, lest that France repent And by disjoining hands hell lose a soul.	The devil wants that, in case France should repent and by releasing his hand hell will lose a soul.
AUSTRIA. King Philip, listen to the Cardinal.	King Philip, listen to the Cardinal.
BASTARD. And hang a calf's-skin on his recreant limbs.	And put a calfskin on his cowardly limbs.
AUSTRIA. Well, ruffian, I must pocket up these wrongs, Because-	Well, scoundrel, I must put these insults in my pocket, because-
BASTARD. Your breeches best may carry them.	Your trousers are the best place for them.

KING JOHN.
Philip, what say'st thou to the Cardinal?

Philip, how will you answer the cardinal?

CONSTANCE.
What should he say, but as the Cardinal?

What can he say, except what the cardinal says?

LEWIS.
Bethink you, father; for the difference
Is purchase of a heavy curse from Rome
Or the light loss of England for a friend.
Forgo the easier.

*Think carefully, father; on the one hand
you could get a heavy curse from Rome,
on the other is the easy loss of England as a friend.
Take the easier course.*

BLANCH.
That's the curse of Rome.

That's accepting the curse of Rome.

CONSTANCE.
O Lewis, stand fast! The devil tempts thee here
In likeness of a new untrimmed bride.

*Oh Louis, be strong! The devil is tempting you,
disguised as a virgin bride.*

BLANCH.
The Lady Constance speaks not from her faith,
But from her need.

*Lady Constance isn't saying what she believes,
she's speaking according to what she wants.*

CONSTANCE.
O, if thou grant my need,
Which only lives but by the death of faith,
That need must needs infer this principle-
That faith would live again by death of need.
O then, tread down my need, and faith mounts up:
Keep my need up, and faith is trodden down!

*O, if you give me what I want,
which I'm only lacking due to faithlessness,
then you must need to think of this—
that faith would live again if the want was
removed. So, give me what I want, and faith
increases: reject me, and you trample on faith.*

KING JOHN.
The King is mov'd, and answers not to this.

The King is disturbed, and doesn't answer this.

CONSTANCE.
O be remov'd from him, and answer well!

Oh, step away from him, and answer well!

AUSTRIA.
Do so, King Philip; hang no more in doubt.

Do so, King Philip; don't stand there doubting.

BASTARD.
Hang nothing but a calf's-skin, most sweet lout.

Dressed in nothing but a calfskin, you sweet lout.

KING PHILIP.
I am perplex'd and know not what to say.

I am confused and don't know what to say.

PANDULPH.
What canst thou say but will perplex thee more,
If thou stand excommunicate and curs'd?

*What if what you say makes you more confused
by making you excommunicated and cursed?*

KING PHILIP.
Good reverend father, make my person yours,
And tell me how you would bestow yourself.
This royal hand and mine are newly knit,
And the conjunction of our inward souls
Married in league, coupled and link'd together
With all religious strength of sacred vows;
The latest breath that gave the sound of words
Was deep-sworn faith, peace, amity, true love,
Between our kingdoms and our royal selves;
And even before this truce, but new before,
No longer than we well could wash our hands,
To clap this royal bargain up of peace,
Heaven knows, they were besmear'd and overstain'd
With slaughter's pencil, where revenge did paint
The fearful difference of incensed kings.
And shall these hands, so lately purg'd of blood,
So newly join'd in love, so strong in both,
Unyoke this seizure and this kind regreet?
Play fast and loose with faith? so jest with heaven,
Make such unconstant children of ourselves,
As now again to snatch our palm from palm,
Unswear faith sworn, and on the marriage-bed
Of smiling peace to march a bloody host,
And make a riot on the gentle brow
Of true sincerity? O, holy sir,
My reverend father, let it not be so!
Out of your grace, devise, ordain, impose,
Some gentle order; and then we shall be blest
To do your pleasure, and continue friends.

PANDULPH.
All form is formless, order orderless,
Save what is opposite to England's love.
Therefore, to arms! be champion of our church,
Or let the church, our mother, breathe her curse-
A mother's curse-on her revolting son.
France, thou mayst hold a serpent by the tongue,
A chafed lion by the mortal paw,
A fasting tiger safer by the tooth,
Than keep in peace that hand which thou dost hold.

KING PHILIP.
I may disjoin my hand, but not my faith.

PANDULPH.
So mak'st thou faith an enemy to faith;

Good reverend father, put yourself in my position, and tell me how you would behave. I have only just joined hands with this King, and our souls have been joined together, sworn to work for each other with all the religious strength of sacred vows; the last thing that I have said was to swear faithfully to peace, friendship and true love between our kingdoms and ourselves. And just before this truce, just recently, no sooner than we could wash our hands to seal this royal bargain of peace, heaven knows, they were smeared and stained with the blood of slaughter, revenge showing how terrible disagreement is between angry kings: should these hands, so recently cleansed of blood, so newly joined in friendship, both so faithful, undo their clasp and their kind bond? Cheat with faith? Should we joke with heaven, be such unfaithful children of God that we would now take our hands apart, unswear what we have sworn, and on the marriage bed of sweet peace march a bloody army, and cause a riot on the gentle forehead of true sincerity? Oh, holy Sir, my reverend father, don't make me do this! From your grace invent, decree, impose some less strict order, and then we will have the blessing of doing as you wish and remaining friends.

All ceremony is powerless, there is no order except in being the opposite of friends with England. So, to battle! Be the champion of our church, or let the church, our mother, say her curse– a mother's curse–against her revolting son. France, you would be safer holding a snake by the tongue, an angry lion by his killing paw, a hungry tiger by his tooth, than to remain at peace with that hand which you are holding.

I can break my grip, but not my promise.

So you are making your promise an enemy of your

And like. a civil war set'st oath to oath.
Thy tongue against thy tongue. O, let thy vow
First made to heaven, first be to heaven perform'd,
That is, to be the champion of our Church.
What since thou swor'st is sworn against thyself
And may not be performed by thyself,
For that which thou hast sworn to do amiss
Is not amiss when it is truly done;
And being not done, where doing tends to ill,
The truth is then most done not doing it;
The better act of purposes mistook
Is to mistake again; though indirect,
Yet indirection thereby grows direct,
And falsehood cures, as fire cools fire
Within the scorched veins of one new-burn'd.
It is religion that doth make vows kept;
But thou hast sworn against religion
By what thou swear'st against the thing thou swear'st,
And mak'st an oath the surety for thy truth
Against an oath; the truth thou art unsure
To swear swears only not to be forsworn;
Else what a mockery should it be to swear!
But thou dost swear only to be forsworn;
And most forsworn to keep what thou dost swear.
Therefore thy later vows against thy first
Is in thyself rebellion to thyself;
And better conquest never canst thou make
Than arm thy constant and thy nobler parts
Against these giddy loose suggestions;
Upon which better part our pray'rs come in,
If thou vouchsafe them. But if not, then know
The peril of our curses fight on thee
So heavy as thou shalt not shake them off,
But in despair die under the black weight.

AUSTRIA.
Rebellion, flat rebellion!

BASTARD.
Will't not be?
Will not a calf's-skin stop that mouth of thine?

LEWIS.
Father, to arms!

BLANCH.
Upon thy wedding-day?
Against the blood that thou hast married?

promise, setting oaths against oaths like a civil war, setting your words against your words. Oh, let your promise which you first made to heaven, be carried out on heaven's behalf, that is, that you would be a champion of our church. Since what you have sworn is swearing against yourself and cannot be done by you, for if you break your oath you are not breaking it if you are doing so to keep your true oath, and not doing something when doing it would be evil then you are being most faithful by not doing it: the best thing to do when you're in the wrong is to do a wrong to right it; although doing wrong you will be doing right by doing wrong, and falsehood will cure falsehood, as fire cools fire in the scorched brains of someone who's just been burned. It is your religion which makes you want to keep your vows, but you have sworn against religion: you are swearing against the thing you have sworn, you are swearing against your own truth! Having sworn an oath you have the effrontery to say that your oath is the guarantee of your truthfulness! This makes a mockery of swearing, doesn't it? But you have sworn only that you won't break your oath, and your oath says that you must keep to what you have sworn. So your later promise goes against your first and so you are fighting against yourself; you can never win a greater victory than if you make sure your true and noble qualities resist the temptation of foolish suggestions. then the prayers of your better part will be answered, if you make them. But if you don't, then you should note that you will be so heavily cursed by us that you will not be able to escape them, and you will die in despair under their black weight.

Rebellion, plain rebellion!

Is everything in vain?
Wouldn't a calfskin block up your mouth?

Father, we must fight!

On your wedding day?
Against the family you have married into?

What, shall our feast be kept with slaughtered men?
Shall braying trumpets and loud churlish drums,
Clamours of hell, be measures to our pomp?
O husband, hear me! ay, alack, how new
Is 'husband' in my mouth! even for that name,
Which till this time my tongue did ne'er pronounce,
Upon my knee I beg, go not to arms
Against mine uncle.

CONSTANCE.
O, upon my knee,
Made hard with kneeling, I do pray to thee,
Thou virtuous Dauphin, alter not the doom
Forethought by heaven!

BLANCH.
Now shall I see thy love. What motive may
Be stronger with thee than the name of wife?

CONSTANCE.
That which upholdeth him that thee upholds,
His honour. O, thine honour, Lewis, thine honour!

LEWIS.
I muse your Majesty doth seem so cold,
When such profound respects do pull you on.

PANDULPH.
I will denounce a curse upon his head.

KING PHILIP.
Thou shalt not need. England, I will fall from thee.

CONSTANCE.
O fair return of banish'd majesty!

ELINOR.
O foul revolt of French inconstancy!

KING JOHN.
France, thou shalt rue this hour within this hour.

BASTARD.
Old Time the clock-setter, that bald sexton Time,
Is it as he will? Well then, France shall rue.

BLANCH.
The sun's o'ercast with blood. Fair day, adieu!

What, shall we celebrate with men's deaths? Shall our wedding music be braying trumpets and loud spiteful drums, the racket of hell? Oh husband, listen to me! Alas, how new that word "husband" is to me! Just because of that name, which I have not ever said until now, I go down on my knees and beg you not to fight against my uncle.

Oh, on my knees, which are worn out with begging, I pray you, you good Dauphin, do not go against the wishes of heaven!

Now I will see what your love is worth. What is more important to you than what your wife asks?

The thing which supports the man who supports you, his honour. Oh, your honour, Louis, your honour!

I'm surprised that your Majesty seems so cold, when such deep considerations should be working on you.

I will announce a curse upon his head.

You won't have to. England, I forsake you.

Here is the fair return of your forgotten majesty!

Disgusting rebellion of French inconstancy!

France, you shall regret what you have done here at once.

Old Father Time, that old gravedigger, is this what he wants? Well then, France will regret this.

The sun has gone bloody red. Farewell, sweet day!

Which is the side that I must go withal?
I am with both: each army hath a hand;
And in their rage, I having hold of both,
They whirl asunder and dismember me.
Husband, I cannot pray that thou mayst win;
Uncle, I needs must pray that thou mayst lose;
Father, I may not wish the fortune thine;
Grandam, I will not wish thy wishes thrive.
Whoever wins, on that side shall I lose:
Assured loss before the match be play'd.

LEWIS.
Lady, with me, with me thy fortune lies.

BLANCH.
There where my fortune lives, there my life dies.

KING JOHN.
Cousin, go draw our puissance together.

Exit

BASTARD
France, I am burn'd up with inflaming wrath,
A rage whose heat hath this condition
That nothing can allay, nothing but blood,
The blood, and dearest-valu'd blood, of France.

KING PHILIP.
Thy rage shall burn thee up, and thou shalt turn
To ashes, ere our blood shall quench that fire.
Look to thyself, thou art in jeopardy.

KING JOHN.
No more than he that threats. To arms let's hie!

Exeunt severally

---

*Which side am I supposed to choose?
I am with both of them: each army claims me;
and in their anger, as I have hold of both their
hands, they will tear me apart.
Husband, I cannot pray that you will win;
uncle, I must pray that you will lose;
father, I don't want you to succeed;
grandmother, I don't want you to get your wishes.
Whoever wins, I shall be the loser:
my loss is guaranteed before the match is even
played.*

Lady, come with me, your fate is with me.

Then where my fate goes, that's where my life dies.

Cousin, let's go and muster our forces.

*France, I am consumed with a burning anger,
an anger whose heat cannot be
cooled by anything except blood,
the blood, the blood of the greatest price, of
France.*

*Your rage will burn you up, and you shall turn
to ashes, before my blood puts that fire out.
Watch out for yourself, you are in danger.*

*In no more danger than the one who threatens it.
Let's arm ourselves!*

SCENE 2.

France. Plains near Angiers

Alarums, excursions. Enter the BASTARD with AUSTRIA'S head

BASTARD.
Now, by my life, this day grows wondrous hot;
Some airy devil hovers in the sky
And pours down mischief. Austria's head lie there,
While Philip breathes.

Now, I swear, the day is growing terribly hot; some flying devil is hovering in the sky and pouring down mischief. Austria, lie your head there, while Philip catches his breath.

Enter KING JOHN, ARTHUR, and HUBERT

KING JOHN.
Hubert, keep this boy. Philip, make up:
My mother is assailed in our tent,
And ta'en, I fear.

Hubert, look after this boy. Philip, get to the front: my mother has been attacked in our tent, and captured, I fear.

BASTARD.
My lord, I rescued her;
Her Highness is in safety, fear you not;
But on, my liege, for very little pains
Will bring this labour to an happy end.

My lord, I rescued her; her Highness is safe, don't worry; but let's go forward, my lord, for a little effort will finish this work successfully.

Exeunt

SCENE 3.

France. Plains near Angiers

Alarums, excursions, retreat. Enter KING JOHN, ELINOR, ARTHUR, the BASTARD, HUBERT, and LORDS

KING JOHN.
[To ELINOR]So shall it be; your Grace shall stay behind,
So strongly guarded.[To ARTHUR]Cousin, look not sad;
Thy grandam loves thee, and thy uncle will
As dear be to thee as thy father was.

This is how it will be; your Grace will stay behind, with this strong guard. Cousin, do not look sad; your grandmother loves you, and your uncle will be as dear to you as your father was.

ARTHUR.
O, this will make my mother die with grief!

Oh, this will make my mother die of grief!

KING JOHN.
[To the BASTARD]Cousin, away for England! haste before,
And, ere our coming, see thou shake the bags
Of hoarding abbots; imprisoned angels
Set at liberty; the fat ribs of peace
Must by the hungry now be fed upon.
Use our commission in his utmost force.

Cousin, let's go to England! You hurry ahead, and, before we get there, make sure you impose taxes on the hoarding abbots; set their coins free; the animals which were fed in peace must now make food for the hungry. Use my full authority.

BASTARD.
Bell, book, and candle, shall not drive me back,
When gold and silver becks me to come on.
I leave your Highness. Grandam, I will pray,
If ever I remember to be holy,
For your fair safety. So, I kiss your hand.

The threat of excommunication will not repel me, when gold and silver is urging me to go on. I take my leave of your Highness. Grandmother, I will pray, if ever I remember to be pious, for your safety. So, I kiss your hand.

ELINOR.
Farewell, gentle cousin.

Farewell, sweet cousin.

KING JOHN.
Coz, farewell.

Cousin, farewell.

Exit BASTARD

ELINOR.
Come hither, little kinsman; hark, a word.

Come here, little relative; listen to me.

KING JOHN.
Come hither, Hubert. O my gentle Hubert,
We owe thee much! Within this wall of flesh
There is a soul counts thee her creditor,

Come here, Hubert. Oh my sweet Hubert, we owe you a lot! Inside this body there is a soul which feels indebted to you,

And with advantage means to pay thy love;
And, my good friend, thy voluntary oath
Lives in this bosom, dearly cherished.
Give me thy hand. I had a thing to say-
But I will fit it with some better time.
By heaven, Hubert, I am almost asham'd
To say what good respect I have of thee.

HUBERT.
I am much bounden to your Majesty.

KING JOHN.
Good friend, thou hast no cause to say so yet,
But thou shalt have; and creep time ne'er so slow,
Yet it shall come for me to do thee good.
I had a thing to say-but let it go:
The sun is in the heaven, and the proud day,
Attended with the pleasures of the world,
Is all too wanton and too full of gawds
To give me audience. If the midnight bell
Did with his iron tongue and brazen mouth
Sound on into the drowsy race of night;
If this same were a churchyard where we stand,
And thou possessed with a thousand wrongs;
Or if that surly spirit, melancholy,
Had bak'd thy blood and made it heavy-thick,
Which else runs tickling up and down the veins,
Making that idiot, laughter, keep men's eyes
And strain their cheeks to idle merriment,
A passion hateful to my purposes;
Or if that thou couldst see me without eyes,
Hear me without thine ears, and make reply
Without a tongue, using conceit alone,
Without eyes, ears, and harmful sound of words-
Then, in despite of brooded watchful day,
I would into thy bosom pour my thoughts.
But, ah, I will not! Yet I love thee well;
And, by my troth, I think thou lov'st me well.

HUBERT.
So well that what you bid me undertake,
Though that my death were adjunct to my act,
By heaven, I would do it.

KING JOHN.
Do not I know thou wouldst?
Good Hubert, Hubert, Hubert, throw thine eye
On yon young boy. I'll tell thee what, my friend,
He is a very serpent in my way;

*and intends to return your love with interest;
and, my good friend, your voluntary promise
lives in my heart, greatly valued.
Give me your hand. I had something to say-
but I will find a better time to say it.
By heaven, Hubert, I am almost embarrassed
to say how well I think of you.*

I'm very indebted to your Majesty.

*Good friend, you have no reason to say so yet,
but you will have; and however slowly time goes,
a time shall arrive when I can do you good.
I was going to say something-but let it go:
the sun is in the sky, and the proud day,
with all the pleasures of the world around it,
is too busy and full of showy ornaments
for me to be listened to: if the midnight bell
with his iron clapper and bronze casing
was ringing in the sleepy hours of the night;
if this was a churchyard where we are standing,
and you were possessed by a thousand evils;
or if that horrid spirit, depression,
had baked your blood and made it heavy, thick,
when otherwise it runs tickling up and down the
veins, making foolish laughter occupy men's eyes
and strain their cheeks in idle merriment,
an emotion which is unsuited to my purpose;
for if you could see me without eyes,
hear me without your ears, and reply
without the time, just using your thoughts,
without eyes, ears, and the harmful sound of
words; then, in spite of the brooding all seeing day,
I would pour my thoughts into your heart:
but, ah, I will not. But I love you well;
and, I swear, I think you love me well.*

*So well that whatever you told me to do,
even if it would cause my death,
I swear that I would do it.*

*Don't I know that you would?
Good Hubert, Hubert, Hubert, look over
at that young boy. I tell you what, my friend,
he is a snake on my path;*

50

And wheresoe'er this foot of mine doth tread,
He lies before me. Dost thou understand me?
Thou art his keeper.

HUBERT.
And I'll keep him so
That he shall not offend your Majesty.

KING JOHN.
Death.

HUBERT.
My lord?

KING JOHN.
A grave.

HUBERT.
He shall not live.

KING JOHN.
Enough!
I could be merry now. Hubert, I love thee.
Well, I'll not say what I intend for thee.
Remember. Madam, fare you well;
I'll send those powers o'er to your Majesty.

ELINOR.
My blessing go with thee!

KING JOHN.
[To ARTHUR]For England, cousin, go;
Hubert shall be your man, attend on you
With all true duty. On toward Calais, ho!

Exeunt

*and wherever I walk
he lies in my way. Do you understand me?
You are his keeper.*

*And I'll keep him in a way
that will stop him offending your Majesty.*

Death.

My lord?

A grave.

He shall not live.

*Good!
I could be merry now. Hubert, I love you.
Well, I won't say what I've got planned for you.
Remember. Madam, Farewell;
I'll send those forces over to your Majesty.*

Take my blessings with you!

*Head for England, cousin;
Hubert will be your servant, he'll
take good care of you. Off you go to Calais!*

SCENE 4.

France. The FRENCH KING's camp

Enter KING PHILIP, LEWIS, PANDULPH, and attendants

KING PHILIP.
So by a roaring tempest on the flood
A whole armado of convicted sail
Is scatter'd and disjoin'd from fellowship.

So a whole armada of doomed ships has been scattered and separated by a roaring storm on the sea.

PANDULPH.
Courage and comfort! All shall yet go well.

Be brave and be calm! Everything will still turn out well.

KING PHILIP.
What can go well, when we have run so ill.
Are we not beaten? Is not Angiers lost?
Arthur ta'en prisoner? Divers dear friends slain?
And bloody England into England gone,
O'erbearing interruption, spite of France?

How can things go well, when we have done so badly? Haven't we been beaten? Hasn't Angiers been lost? Arthur taken prisoner? Many dear friends killed? And the bloody king of England gone back to England, brushing aside our interventions, to spite France?

LEWIS.
What he hath won, that hath he fortified;
So hot a speed with such advice dispos'd,
Such temperate order in so fierce a cause,
Doth want example; who hath read or heard
Of any kindred action like to this?

He has fortified the towns he has won; doing such things with such urgent speed, being so organised and at the same time so energetic, is unheard of; has anybody ever read or heard of such a thing?

KING PHILIP.
Well could I bear that England had this praise,
So we could find some pattern of our shame.

I wouldn't mind England being praised for this, if we could find anyone who had ever been as shamed as us.

Enter CONSTANCE

[Enter Constance]

Look who comes here! a grave unto a soul;
Holding th' eternal spirit, against her will,
In the vile prison of afflicted breath.
I prithee, lady, go away with me.

Look who's coming! The grave of a soul; the eternal spirit is being kept against her will in the vile prison of the body. I beg you, lady, come away with me.

CONSTANCE.
Lo now! now see the issue of your peace!

Look now! Now see how your peace has turned out!

KING PHILIP.
Patience, good lady! Comfort, gentle Constance!

Be patient, good lady! Be calm, sweet Constance!

CONSTANCE.
No, I defy all counsel, all redress,
But that which ends all counsel, true redress-
Death, death; O amiable lovely death!

No, I refuse all advice, all repayment, except that which owns all advice, true repayment- death, death; oh friendly, lovely death!

Thou odoriferous stench! sound rottenness!
Arise forth from the couch of lasting night,
Thou hate and terror to prosperity,
And I will kiss thy detestable bones,
And put my eyeballs in thy vaulty brows,
And ring these fingers with thy household worms,
And stop this gap of breath with fulsome dust,
And be a carrion monster like thyself.
Come, grin on me, and I will think thou smil'st,
And buss thee as thy wife. Misery's love,
O, come to me!

KING PHILIP.
O fair affliction, peace!

CONSTANCE.
No, no, I will not, having breath to cry.
O that my tongue were in the thunder's mouth!
Then with a passion would I shake the world,
And rouse from sleep that fell anatomy
Which cannot hear a lady's feeble voice,
Which scorns a modern invocation.

PANDULPH.
Lady, you utter madness and not sorrow.

CONSTANCE.
Thou art holy to belie me so.
I am not mad: this hair I tear is mine;
My name is Constance; I was Geffrey's wife;
Young Arthur is my son, and he is lost.
I am not mad—I would to heaven I were!
For then 'tis like I should forget myself.
O, if I could, what grief should I forget!
Preach some philosophy to make me mad,
And thou shalt be canoniz'd, Cardinal;
For, being not mad, but sensible of grief,
My reasonable part produces reason
How I may be deliver'd of these woes,
And teaches me to kill or hang myself.
If I were mad I should forget my son,
Or madly think a babe of clouts were he.
I am not mad; too well, too well I feel
The different plague of each calamity.

KING PHILIP.
Bind up those tresses. O, what love I note
In the fair multitude of those her hairs!
Where but by a chance a silver drop hath fall'n,

*You reeking stench! Solid rottenness!
Rise up from the eternal night,
you hated terror of prosperity,
and I will kiss your revolting bones,
and put my eyeballs into your skull,
and wear your household worms as rings,
and stop my gasping breath with nauseous dust,
and be a rotting monster like yourself.
Come, grin at me, and I will think you are smiling,
and kiss you as your wife. Lover of misery,
oh, come to me!*

Oh lovely torment, peace!

*No, no, I will not be quiet, as long as I have breath
to cry. I wish that I could speak like thunder!
Then I would shake the world with a passion,
and wake that cruel skeleton from its sleep
which cannot hear the feeble voice of a lady,
which scorns modern spells.*

Lady, this is not sorrow, this is madness.

*It's very holy of you to portray me as such.
I am not mad: this hair I tear is my own;
my name is Constance; I was the wife of Geoffrey;
young Arthur is my son, and he has been lost.
I am not mad—I wish to heaven I was!
For then I would be able to forget who I am,
oh, if I could, what grief I would be forgetting!
Tell me how I can turn myself mad,
and you will be canonised, Cardinal;
for, not being mad but able to feel grief,
my mind offers me the solution
to help me escape from my sorrows,
and tells me to kill or hang myself.
If I were mad I would forget about my son,
or madly think that he was worthless.
I am not mad; I can feel the curse of each
terrible event all too well.*

*Tie up your hair. Oh, what love I can see
in that lovely crop of her hair!
When a silver tear has fallen there by chance*

Even to that drop ten thousand wiry friends
Do glue themselves in sociable grief,
Like true, inseparable, faithful loves,
Sticking together in calamity.

CONSTANCE.
To England, if you will.

KING PHILIP.
Bind up your hairs.

CONSTANCE.
Yes, that I will; and wherefore will I do it?
I tore them from their bonds, and cried aloud
'O that these hands could so redeem my son,
As they have given these hairs their liberty!'
But now I envy at their liberty,
And will again commit them to their bonds,
Because my poor child is a prisoner.
And, father Cardinal, I have heard you say
That we shall see and know our friends in heaven;
If that be true, I shall see my boy again;
For since the birth of Cain, the first male child,
To him that did but yesterday suspire,
There was not such a gracious creature born.
But now will canker sorrow eat my bud
And chase the native beauty from his cheek,
And he will look as hollow as a ghost,
As dim and meagre as an ague's fit;
And so he'll die; and, rising so again,
When I shall meet him in the court of heaven
I shall not know him. Therefore never, never
Must I behold my pretty Arthur more.

PANDULPH.
You hold too heinous a respect of grief.

CONSTANCE.
He talks to me that never had a son.

KING PHILIP.
You are as fond of grief as of your child.

CONSTANCE.
Grief fills the room up of my absent child,
Lies in his bed, walks up and down with me,
Puts on his pretty looks, repeats his words,
Remembers me of all his gracious parts,
Stuffs out his vacant garments with his form;

*ten thousand wiry friends glue themselves to it,
sharing in its grief,
like true, inseparable, faithful lovers,
sticking together through disaster.*

Let's go to England, if you agree.

Tie up your hair.

*Yes, I shall; and why will I do it?
I tore them from their constraints, and cried aloud
"I wish these hands could free my son as easily
as they have freed these hairs!"
But now I am jealous of their freedom,
and will tie them up again,
because my poor child is a prisoner.
And, Father Cardinal, I have heard you say
that we will see and recognise our friends in
heaven; if that is true, I will see my boy again;
for since Cain, the first male child, was born,
up until the last boy born yesterday,
there was never such a lovely creature born.
But now the disease of sorrow eats at my bud
and drives the natural beauty out of his face,
and he will look as thin as a ghost,
as grey and skinny as one with a fever;
and so he will die; and, rising up again,
when I meet him in heaven
I will not recognise him. So I will never, never
ever see my pretty Arthur again.*

It's sinful to have such respect for grief.

The one who talks to me has never had a son.

You like your grief as much as your child.

*Grief fills up the room of my absent child,
lies in his bed, walks up and down with me,
imitates his looks, speaks like him,
reminds me of all his good qualities,
fills his empty clothes with his shape;*

Then have I reason to be fond of grief. Fare you well; had you such a loss as I, I could give better comfort than you do. I will not keep this form upon my head, [Tearing her hair] When there is such disorder in my wit. O Lord! my boy, my Arthur, my fair son! My life, my joy, my food, my ail the world! My widow-comfort, and my sorrows' cure!	*so I have good reason to like grief. Farewell; if you had suffered my loss, I would be able to comfort you better than you comfort me. I won't keep my hair in order, when my mind is so disordered. Oh Lord! My boy, my Arthur, my lovely son! My life, my joy, my food, my whole world! The comfort of my widowhood, cure of all my sorrows!*

Exit

KING PHILIP.
I fear some outrage, and I'll follow her.	*I'm afraid she'll do herself some damage, and I will follow her.*

Exit

LEWIS.
There's nothing in this world can make me joy. Life is as tedious as a twice-told tale Vexing the dull ear of a drowsy man; And bitter shame hath spoil'd the sweet world's taste, That it yields nought but shame and bitterness.	*There's nothing in this world which can make me happy. Life is as dull as a story you've heard already irritating the unhearing ear of a sleepy man; bitter shame has spoilt the sweet taste of the world, so that I can taste only shame and bitterness.*

PANDULPH.
Before the curing of a strong disease, Even in the instant of repair and health, The fit is strongest; evils that take leave On their departure most of all show evil; What have you lost by losing of this day?	*Before a strong disease can be cured, even at the moment that health is returning, it is at its worst; evils that can be seen as they leave are the most evil; what have you lost by your defeat today?*

LEWIS.
All days of glory, joy, and happiness.	*Any chance of glory, joy and happiness.*

PANDULPH.
If you had won it, certainly you had. No, no; when Fortune means to men most good, She looks upon them with a threat'ning eye. 'Tis strange to think how much King John hath lost In this which he accounts so clearly won. Are not you griev'd that Arthur is his prisoner?	*If you had one, you certainly would have. No, no; when Fortune intends to favour men most, she looks at them frighteningly. It's strange to think how much King John has lost in this action which he thinks he has obviously won. Aren't you upset that Arthur is his prisoner?*

LEWIS.
As heartily as he is glad he hath him.	*As much as he is glad to have captured him.*

PANDULPH.
Your mind is all as youthful as your blood.	*Your mind is as immature as your body.*

Now hear me speak with a prophetic spirit;
For even the breath of what I mean to speak
Shall blow each dust, each straw, each little rub,
Out of the path which shall directly lead
Thy foot to England's throne. And therefore mark:
John hath seiz'd Arthur; and it cannot be
That, whiles warm life plays in that infant's veins,
The misplac'd John should entertain an hour,
One minute, nay, one quiet breath of rest.
A sceptre snatch'd with an unruly hand
Must be boisterously maintain'd as gain'd,
And he that stands upon a slipp'ry place
Makes nice of no vile hold to stay him up;
That John may stand then, Arthur needs must fall;
So be it, for it cannot be but so.

LEWIS.
But what shall I gain by young Arthur's fall?

PANDULPH.
You, in the right of Lady Blanch your wife,
May then make all the claim that Arthur did.

LEWIS.
And lose it, life and all, as Arthur did.

PANDULPH.
How green you are and fresh in this old world!
John lays you plots; the times conspire with you;
For he that steeps his safety in true blood
Shall find but bloody safety and untrue.
This act, so evilly borne, shall cool the hearts
Of all his people and freeze up their zeal,
That none so small advantage shall step forth
To check his reign but they will cherish it;
No natural exhalation in the sky,
No scope of nature, no distemper'd day,
No common wind, no customed event,
But they will pluck away his natural cause
And call them meteors, prodigies, and signs,
Abortives, presages, and tongues of heaven,
Plainly denouncing vengeance upon John.

LEWIS.
May be he will not touch young Arthur's life,
But hold himself safe in his prisonment.

PANDULPH.
O, Sir, when he shall hear of your approach,

Now listen to me prophesy;
just the breath of what I say
will blow each bit of dust, each straw, each little
obstacle, out of the path which leads directly for
you on to the throne of England. And so note this:
John has captured Arthur; while that child
has any warm blood in his veins it cannot be
that thieving John can ever enjoy an hour,
a minute, no, not one quiet breath of rest.
When a sceptre has been snatched by violence
it must be kept with the same energy with which it
was gained, and someone who is standing in a
slippery place does not reject any evil which will
keep him upright. So that John can stand, Arthur
has to fall; this will happen, it's the only thing that
can happen.

But what will I gain by young Arthur's fall?

You can claim everything that Arthur did
through your rights as husband of Lady Blanche.

And lose it, along with my life, as Arthur did.

How innocent you are to the ways of this old
world! John plots against you; the times are on
your side; for someone who sheds noble blood for
his own safety will find that safety is bloody and
unsafe. When he does this evil act it will cool the
hearts of all his people and take away their
passion, so that when any small opportunity arises
to stop his rule they will welcome it;
there will be no natural cloud in the sky,
no natural event, no stormy day,
no ordinary wind, no normal happening,
without them ignoring the natural cause
and calling them meteors, unnatural signs,
abortions, predictions, voices from heaven,
plainly proclaiming that John must be punished.

Maybe he will not kill young Arthur,
but keep himself safe by imprisoning him.

Oh sir, when he hears that you are coming,

If that young Arthur be not gone already,
Even at that news he dies; and then the hearts
Of all his people shall revolt from him,
And kiss the lips of unacquainted change,
And pick strong matter of revolt and wrath
Out of the bloody fingers' ends of John.
Methinks I see this hurly all on foot;
And, O, what better matter breeds for you
Than I have nam'd! The bastard Faulconbridge
Is now in England ransacking the Church,
Offending charity; if but a dozen French
Were there in arms, they would be as a call
To train ten thousand English to their side;
Or as a little snow, tumbled about,
Anon becomes a mountain. O noble Dauphin,
Go with me to the King. 'Tis wonderful
What may be wrought out of their discontent,
Now that their souls are topful of offence.
For England go; I will whet on the King.

LEWIS.
Strong reasons makes strange actions. Let us go;
If you say ay, the King will not say no.

Exeunt

*if young Arthur has not already being killed,
he will be killed at the news; and then the hearts
of all his people will revolt against him,
and welcome unknown change,
and find good cause for revolution and anger
in John's bloody hands.
I can picture all this chaos;
and how can things go better for you
than what I have described! The bastard
Faulconbridge is stealing money from the church
in England, losing goodwill; if there were just a
dozen Frenchmen there in arms, that would be a
summons that would bring ten thousand
Englishmen to their side; it would be like a little
snow which stirred up soon becomes an avalanche.
O noble Dauphin, come with me to the king. It's
amazing what can be created from unhappiness,
now that their souls are brimful of wrongdoing.
Go to England; I will encourage the King.*

*We must do strange things when we have good
reasons to. Let's go;
if you say yes, the King will not say no.*

Act IV.

SCENE 1.

England. A castle

Enter HUBERT and EXECUTIONERS

HUBERT.
Heat me these irons hot; and look thou stand
Within the arras. When I strike my foot
Upon the bosom of the ground, rush forth
And bind the boy which you shall find with me
Fast to the chair. Be heedful; hence, and watch.

EXECUTIONER.
I hope your warrant will bear out the deed.

HUBERT.
Uncleanly scruples! Fear not you. Look to't.

Exeunt

EXECUTIONERS
Young lad, come forth; I have to say with you.

Enter ARTHUR

ARTHUR.
Good morrow, Hubert.

HUBERT.
Good morrow, little Prince.

ARTHUR.
As little prince, having so great a tide
To be more prince, as may be. You are sad.

HUBERT.
Indeed I have been merrier.

ARTHUR.
Mercy on me!
Methinks no body should be sad but I;
Yet, I remember, when I was in France,
Young gentlemen would be as sad as night,
Only for wantonness. By my christendom,
So I were out of prison and kept sheep,
I should be as merry as the day is long;
And so I would be here but that I doubt

*Heat these irons hot for me; and you go and hide
behind the curtain. When I stamp my foot
upon the floor, rush out
and tie up the boy you find with me
tight to the chair. Keep alert; off you go, and watch
out.*

*I hope that your warrant gives you permission for
this.*

Improper doubts! Don't worry. Get it done.

Young lad, come out; I need to speak with you.

Good morning, Hubert.

Good morning, little Prince.

*I am as small a prince as one who is going to be
such a much greater prince can be. You are sad.*

I have certainly been happier.

*God forgive me!
I imagine that nobody could be sad but me;
but I remember, when I was in France,
young gentlemen would be a sad as night
just for show. I swear by my kingdom,
that if I was out of prison and keeping sheep,
I would be as happy as the day is long;
I would be the same here except for my fear*

My uncle practises more harm to me;
He is afraid of me, and I of him.
Is it my fault that I was Geffrey's son?
No, indeed, ist not; and I would to heaven
I were your son, so you would love me, Hubert.

HUBERT.
[Aside]If I talk to him, with his innocent prate
He will awake my mercy, which lies dead;
Therefore I will be sudden and dispatch.

ARTHUR.
Are you sick, Hubert? You look pale to-day;
In sooth, I would you were a little sick,
That I might sit all night and watch with you.
I warrant I love you more than you do me.

HUBERT.
[Aside]His words do take possession of my bosom.-
Read here, young Arthur.[Showing a paper]
[Aside]How now, foolish rheum!
Turning dispiteous torture out of door!
I must be brief, lest resolution drop
Out at mine eyes in tender womanish tears.-
Can you not read it? Is it not fair writ?

ARTHUR.
Too fairly, Hubert, for so foul effect.
Must you with hot irons burn out both mine eyes?

HUBERT.
Young boy, I must.

ARTHUR.
And will you?

HUBERT.
And I will.

ARTHUR.
Have you the heart? When your head did but ache,
I knit my handkerchief about your brows-
The best I had, a princess wrought it me-
And I did never ask it you again;
And with my hand at midnight held your head;
And, like the watchful minutes to the hour,
Still and anon cheer'd up the heavy time,

*that my uncle means to do me more harm;
he is afraid of me, and I am afraid of him.
Is it my fault that I was Geoffrey's son?
No it certainly isn't; I wish to heaven
that I were your son, Hubert, and that you would
love me.*

*If I talk with him his innocent chatter
will inspire my mercy, which is dead now;
so I will get the business over quickly.*

*Are you ill, Hubert? You look pale today;
I swear, I wish that you were a little ill,
so that I could sit up all night to keep you
company. I believe I love you more than you do me.*

*His words have taken hold of my heart–
Read this, young Arthur.*

*What's this, foolish tears!
Driving dispassionate torture out of the door!
I must be quick, unless my strength falls
out of my eyes in tender effeminate tears–
can't you read it? Isn't it clearly written?*

*To clear, Hubert, for such a dark purpose.
Must you burn both my eyes out with hot irons?*

Young boy, I must.

And will you?

And I will.

*Have you the heart to do it? When you had a
headache, I tied my handkerchief around your
forehead– the best I had, a Princess made it for
me– and I never asked for it back; at midnight I
held your head in my hands; and I tried to cheer up
the dark time and make it past like the minutes in
the hour, saying, "what do you need?" And "where*

60

Saying 'What lack you?' and 'Where lies your grief?'
Or 'What good love may I perform for you?'
Many a poor man's son would have lyen still,
And ne'er have spoke a loving word to you;
But you at your sick service had a prince.
Nay, you may think my love was crafty love,
And call it cunning. Do, an if you will.
If heaven be pleas'd that you must use me ill,
Why, then you must. Will you put out mine eyes,
These eyes that never did nor never shall
So much as frown on you?

HUBERT.
I have sworn to do it;
And with hot irons must I burn them out.

ARTHUR.
Ah, none but in this iron age would do it!
The iron of itself, though heat red-hot,
Approaching near these eyes would drink my tears,
And quench his fiery indignation
Even in the matter of mine innocence;
Nay, after that, consume away in rust
But for containing fire to harm mine eye.
Are you more stubborn-hard than hammer'd iron?
An if an angel should have come to me
And told me Hubert should put out mine eyes,
I would not have believ'd him–no tongue but Hubert's.

HUBERT.
[Stamps]Come forth.

Re-enter EXECUTIONERS, With cord, irons, etc.

Do as I bid you do.

ARTHUR.
O, save me, Hubert, save me! My eyes are out
Even with the fierce looks of these bloody men.

HUBERT.
Give me the iron, I say, and bind him here.

ARTHUR.
Alas, what need you be so boist'rous rough?
I will not struggle, I will stand stone-still.
For heaven sake, Hubert, let me not be bound!

does it hurt?"
Or "is there anything that I can do for you?"
Many sons of poor men would have just slept
and never spoken a loving word to you;
but to serve you in your sickness you had a prince.
Well, you may think that my love was a trick,
and call it cunning. Do, if you want to.
If heaven is determined that you must treat me
badly, well, then you must. Are you going to put out my eyes,
the eyes that never did and never will
so much as frown at you?

I have sworn to do it;
and I must burn them out with hot irons.

Ah, only people in this iron age could do it!
The iron on its own, although heated redhot,
coming near these eyes would drink my tears,
and extinguish its fiery anger
with the stuff of my innocence;
and after that it would rust away
as punishment for having fire to harm my eyes.
Are you more stubborn and hard than forged iron?
If an angel had come to me
and told me that Hubert would put out my eyes,
I wouldn't have believed him–I only believe it when
I hear it from Hubert.

Come out.

Do as I tell you.

Oh save me, Hubert, save me! I am blinded
just by the fierce looks of these bloodthirsty men.

Give me the iron and tie him up here.

Alas, why'd you need to be so terribly rough?
I won't struggle, I'm standing as still as a stone.
For heavens sake, Hubert, don't let them tie me!

Nay, hear me, Hubert! Drive these men away,
And I will sit as quiet as a lamb;
I will not stir, nor wince, nor speak a word,
Nor look upon the iron angrily;
Thrust but these men away, and I'll forgive you,
Whatever torment you do put me to.

HUBERT.
Go, stand within; let me alone with him.

EXECUTIONER.
I am best pleas'd to be from such a deed.

Exeunt EXECUTIONERS

ARTHUR.
Alas, I then have chid away my friend!
He hath a stern look but a gentle heart.
Let him come back, that his compassion may
Give life to yours.

HUBERT.
Come, boy, prepare yourself.

ARTHUR.
Is there no remedy?

HUBERT.
None, but to lose your eyes.

ARTHUR.
O heaven, that there were but a mote in yours,
A grain, a dust, a gnat, a wandering hair,
Any annoyance in that precious sense!
Then, feeling what small things are boisterous there,
Your vile intent must needs seem horrible.

HUBERT.
Is this your promise? Go to, hold your tongue.

ARTHUR.
Hubert, the utterance of a brace of tongues
Must needs want pleading for a pair of eyes.
Let me not hold my tongue, let me not, Hubert;
Or, Hubert, if you will, cut out my tongue,
So I may keep mine eyes. O, spare mine eyes,
Though to no use but still to look on you!
Lo, by my troth, the instrument is cold

No, listen to me, Hubert! Send these men away,
and I will sit as quiet as a lamb;
I will not move, or wince, or say a word,
or look angrily at the iron;
only send these men away and I will forgive you,
whatever torture you put on me.

Go and stand in the next room; leave me alone with him.

I'm well pleased to be excused doing this.

Alas, it seems I have sent away my friend!
He looked stern but had gentle heart.
Bring him back, so his compassion can inspire yours.

Come, boy, get ready.

Is there nothing to be done?

Nothing, you must lose your eyes.

I wish to heaven that there was just a speck in yours,
a grain, dust, a gnat, a stray hair,
any irritation to your eyesight!
Then, feeling how revolting small things there are,
you would see how horrible your evil plan is.

Is that all you have to say? Enough, hold your tongue.

Hubert, the speech of a pair of tongues
is not enough to plead for a pair of eyes.
Don't make me hold my tongue, don't make me,
Hubert; or, Hubert, if you like, cut out my tongue,
and let me keep my eyes. Oh, spare my eyes,
even if just so I can look at you!
Look, I swear, the instrument is cold

And would not harm me.

HUBERT.
I can heat it, boy.

ARTHUR.
No, in good sooth; the fire is dead with grief,
Being create for comfort, to be us'd
In undeserved extremes. See else yourself:
There is no malice in this burning coal;
The breath of heaven hath blown his spirit out,
And strew'd repentant ashes on his head.

HUBERT.
But with my breath I can revive it, boy.

ARTHUR.
An if you do, you will but make it blush
And glow with shame of your proceedings, Hubert.
Nay, it perchance will sparkle in your eyes,
And, like a dog that is compell'd to fight,
Snatch at his master that doth tarre him on.
All things that you should use to do me wrong
Deny their office; only you do lack
That mercy which fierce fire and iron extends,
Creatures of note for mercy lacking uses.

HUBERT.
Well, see to live; I will not touch thine eye
For all the treasure that thine uncle owes.
Yet I am sworn, and I did purpose, boy,
With this same very iron to burn them out.

ARTHUR.
O, now you look like Hubert! All this while
You were disguis'd.

HUBERT.
Peace; no more. Adieu.
Your uncle must not know but you are dead:
I'll fill these dogged spies with false reports;
And, pretty child, sleep doubtless and secure
That Hubert, for the wealth of all the world,
Will not offend thee.

ARTHUR.
O heaven! I thank you, Hubert.

HUBERT.

and cannot harm me.

I can heat it, boy.

*No, by heaven; the fire is dead from grief,
as it was made to comfort us, at being used
in such a terrible way. Look for yourself:
there is no evil in this burning coal;
the breath of heaven has blown out his spirit,
and piled the ashes of repentance on his head.*

But I can bring back to life with my breath, boy.

*If you do, you will only be making it blush
with shame at your behaviour, Hubert.
No, maybe it will sparkle in your eyes,
and, like a dog that is forced to fight,
bite his master who is urging him on.
Everything you want to harm me with
refuses to do so; it's only you who lacks
the mercy which fierce fire and iron offers,
a creature who should be able to show mercy.*

*Well, I must think of what's best; I won't touch your
eyes for all the treasure that your uncle has.
But I swore, and I intended, boy,
to burn them out with this iron here.*

*Oh, now you look like Hubert! All this time
you were disguised.*

*Quiet; no more. Goodbye.
Your uncle must believe that you are dead:
I'll give these cruel spies false reports;
and, pretty child, sleep without fear, safe in the
knowledge that Hubert will not harm you
for all the wealth in the world.*

Oh heaven! I thank you, Hubert.

Silence; no more. Go closely in with me.
Much danger do I undergo for thee.

Exeunt

*Silence; no more. Stick close to me.
I'm taking a great risk for you.*

SCENE 2.

England. KING JOHN'S palace

Enter KING JOHN, PEMBROKE, SALISBURY, and other LORDS

KING JOHN.
Here once again we sit, once again crown'd,
And look'd upon, I hope, with cheerful eyes.

Here I sit once again, once again with my crown, and, I hope, looked upon by happy eyes.

PEMBROKE.
This once again, but that your Highness pleas'd,
Was once superfluous: you were crown'd before,
And that high royalty was ne'er pluck'd off,
The faiths of men ne'er stained with revolt;
Fresh expectation troubled not the land
With any long'd-for change or better state.

To say once again, except that your Highness wished, was unnecessary: you had the crown before, and your great royalty was never taken away, the loyalty of men was never stained with rebellion; the land was not troubled by demands for any desired change or better leader.

SALISBURY.
Therefore, to be possess'd with double pomp,
To guard a title that was rich before,
To gild refined gold, to paint the lily,
To throw a perfume on the violet,
To smooth the ice, or add another hue
Unto the rainbow, or with taper-light
To seek the beauteous eye of heaven to garnish,
Is wasteful and ridiculous excess.

So, to be given a double ceremony, to add to a title that was rich before, to gild refined gold, to paint the lily, to put perfume on a violet, to polish ice, or add another colour to the rainbow, or try to add to the sunlight with the light of a candle, is wasteful and foolishly excessive.

PEMBROKE.
But that your royal pleasure must be done,
This act is as an ancient tale new told
And, in the last repeating, troublesome,
Being urged at a time unseasonable.

Except for your royal insistence, this act is like an old story retold and, in this retelling, it is troublesome, because this is the wrong time for it.

SALISBURY.
In this the antique and well-noted face
Of plain old form is much disfigured;
And like a shifted wind unto a sail
It makes the course of thoughts to fetch about,
Startles and frights consideration,
Makes sound opinion sick, and truth suspected,
For putting on so new a fashion'd robe.

This is disfiguring the ancient and well-known face of the simple old rules, like a changing wind with a sail it makes the course of thoughts change, it disturbs and worries contemplation, makes good opinions seem bad, makes truth seem like lies, putting on such a newly made robe.

PEMBROKE.
When workmen strive to do better than well,
They do confound their skill in covetousness;
And oftentimes excusing of a fault
Doth make the fault the worse by th' excuse,

When workmen try to do better than well, they defeat their own skill in doing so; often trying to repair a fault makes the fault worse when repairing it,

As patches set upon a little breach
Discredit more in hiding of the fault
Than did the fault before it was so patch'd.

SALISBURY.
To this effect, before you were new-crown'd,
We breath'd our counsel; but it pleas'd your Highness
To overbear it; and we are all well pleas'd,
Since all and every part of what we would
Doth make a stand at what your Highness will.

KING JOHN.
Some reasons of this double coronation
I have possess'd you with, and think them strong;
And more, more strong, when lesser is my fear,
I shall indue you with. Meantime but ask
What you would have reform'd that is not well,
And well shall you perceive how willingly
I will both hear and grant you your requests.

PEMBROKE.
Then I, as one that am the tongue of these,
To sound the purposes of all their hearts,
Both for myself and them- but, chief of all,
Your safety, for the which myself and them
Bend their best studies, heartily request
Th' enfranchisement of Arthur, whose restraint
Doth move the murmuring lips of discontent
To break into this dangerous argument:
If what in rest you have in right you hold,
Why then your fears-which, as they say, attend
The steps of wrong-should move you to mew up
Your tender kinsman, and to choke his days
With barbarous ignorance, and deny his youth
The rich advantage of good exercise?
That the time's enemies may not have this
To grace occasions, let it be our suit
That you have bid us ask his liberty;
Which for our goods we do no further ask
Than whereupon our weal, on you depending,
Counts it your weal he have his liberty.

KING JOHN.
Let it be so. I do commit his youth
To your direction.

Enter HUBERT

*like patches put on a little damage
which look worse in trying to hide it
than the damage did before it was patched.*

*This is what we advised you before
you were crowned for the second time; but your Highness
decided to overrule us; and we were all well
pleased, since everything that we want and believe
must be matched with what your Highness decides.*

*I have given you some reasons for this
second coronation, and I think they are good ones;
and when my fear is lessened I will give you more,
stronger ones. Meanwhile just say
what you think is not good and want changed,
and you will see clearly how willing I am
both to hear and to grant your requests.*

*Then, as I'm the spokesman for all of these,
and know what they think in their hearts,
both for myself and for them, but chiefly
for your safety, which myself and them
do everything they can for, heartily request
that Arthur should be freed: his imprisonment
is making the whispers of discontent
erupt into a dangerous argument:
if you have a right to all your possessions,
then why are you so afraid, which they say is
a sign of wrong doing, that you imprison
your young kinsman, and suffocate him
with a lack of education, and refuse his youth
the great benefits of good exercise?
So that your enemies at this time cannot have
this to use as an excuse, let the request you told us
to make be that you give him his freedom;
we only ask this for our own good insofar as
our good depends on your good,
and it will do you good to set him free.*

*Let it be so. I entrust this youth
to your guardianship.*

[Aside] Hubert, what news with you?

PEMBROKE.
This is the man should do the bloody deed:
He show'd his warrant to a friend of mine;
The image of a wicked heinous fault
Lives in his eye; that close aspect of his
Doth show the mood of a much troubled breast,
And I do fearfully believe 'tis done
What we so fear'd he had a charge to do.

SALISBURY.
The colour of the King doth come and go
Between his purpose and his conscience,
Like heralds 'twixt two dreadful battles set.
His passion is so ripe it needs must break.

PEMBROKE.
And when it breaks, I fear will issue thence
The foul corruption of a sweet child's death.

KING JOHN.
We cannot hold mortality's strong hand.
Good lords, although my will to give is living,
The suit which you demand is gone and dead:
He tells us Arthur is deceas'd to-night.

SALISBURY.
Indeed, we fear'd his sickness was past cure.

PEMBROKE.
Indeed, we heard how near his death he was,
Before the child himself felt he was sick.
This must be answer'd either here or hence.

KING JOHN.
Why do you bend such solemn brows on me?
Think you I bear the shears of destiny?
Have I commandment on the pulse of life?

SALISBURY.
It is apparent foul-play; and 'tis shame
That greatness should so grossly offer it.
So thrive it in your game! and so, farewell.

PEMBROKE.
Stay yet, Lord Salisbury, I'll go with thee
And find th' inheritance of this poor child,
His little kingdom of a forced grave.

Hubert, what's the news?

This is the man who should have done the bloody deed: he showed his warrant to a friend of mine; the look in his eye shows that he has committed some terrible wicked sin; that stern face of his reveals the mood of a very troubled heart, and I fear that he has performed the thing which we were so afraid he had been ordered to do.

The King's face goes red and pale, alternating between his desires and his conscience, like heralds running between two terrible armies. He's so full of passion he must explode.

And when he does, I fear that out of him will come the revolting stench of the death of a sweet child.

We cannot stop the strong hand of death. Good lords, although I still want to give you what you want, what you asked for is dead and gone: he has told me that Arthur died tonight.

Indeed, we were afraid his illness was incurable.

Indeed, we heard how near death he was, before the child even thought he was ill. This must be answered for either here or in future.

Why are you frowning at me like that? Do think that I have influence over destiny? Do I control the pulse of life?

It is obvious foul play; and it's shameful that one of the great should do such a horrible thing.
May you get what you deserve! And so, farewell.

Wait, Lord Salisbury, I'll go with you and find the inheritance of this poor child, his little kingdom of his early grave.

That blood which ow'd the breadth of all this isle Three foot of it doth hold-bad world the while! This must not be thus borne: this will break out To all our sorrows, and ere long I doubt.	*The lad who had a right to this whole island has just three feet of it —what a wicked world! This must not be tolerated: it will be revealed to all our detriment, and before long I'm sure.*

Exeunt LORDS

KING JOHN. They burn in indignation. I repent. There is no sure foundation set on blood, No certain life achiev'd by others' death.	*They burn with indignation. I repent. There is no solid foundation to be found in blood, no certainty of life to be found in the death of others.*

Enter a MESSENGER

[Enter a messenger]

A fearful eye thou hast; where is that blood That I have seen inhabit in those cheeks? So foul a sky clears not without a storm. Pour down thy weather-how goes all in France?	*You look scared; where is the blood that I have seen filling those cheeks? A foul sky like this won't clear without a storm, let it all pour out–what's happening in France?*
MESSENGER. From France to England. Never such a pow'r For any foreign preparation Was levied in the body of a land. The copy of your speed is learn'd by them, For when you should be told they do prepare, The tidings comes that they are all arriv'd.	*France is coming to England. No country ever raised such a force for a foreign expedition. They have learned from copying your speed, so that when you are told that they are preparing you will get the news that they have arrived.*
KING JOHN. O, where hath our intelligence been drunk? Where hath it slept? Where is my mother's care, That such an army could be drawn in France, And she not hear of it?	*Oh, where have our spies been drunk? Where did they sleep? How careless has my mother been, that such an army could be raised in France, and her not hear of it?*
MESSENGER. My liege, her ear Is stopp'd with dust: the first of April died Your noble mother; and as I hear, my lord, The Lady Constance in a frenzy died Three days before; but this from rumour's tongue I idly heard-if true or false I know not.	*My lord, her ears are blocked with dust: your noble mother died on the first of April; and I have heard, my lord, the Lady Constance died in a fit three days before; but I heard this from idle gossip–I don't know if it's true or false.*
KING JOHN. Withhold thy speed, dreadful occasion! O, make a league with me, till I have pleas'd My discontented peers! What! mother dead! How wildly then walks my estate in France! Under whose conduct came those pow'rs of France That thou for truth giv'st out are landed here?	*Disaster, don't rush on so quickly! Make peace with me, until I have pacified my unhappy peers! What! Mother dead! How unruly then my lands in France are! Who is leading those French forces that you tell me have landed here?*

MESSENGER.
Under the Dauphin.

They are led by the Dauphin.

KING JOHN.
Thou hast made me giddy
With these ill tidings.

*You have made me dizzy
with all this bad news.*

Enter the BASTARD and PETER OF POMFRET

[Enter the Bastard and Peter of Pomfret]

Now! What says the world
To your proceedings? Do not seek to stuff
My head with more ill news, for it is full.

*Now! What news do you have
of your business? Don't try and put
more bad news in my head, because it's full.*

BASTARD.
But if you be afear'd to hear the worst,
Then let the worst, unheard, fall on your head.

*But if you're afraid to hear the worst,
then let the worst, unheard, fall on your head.*

KING JOHN.
Bear with me, cousin, for I was amaz'd
Under the tide; but now I breathe again
Aloft the flood, and can give audience
To any tongue, speak it of what it will.

*Bear with me cousin, I was overwhelmed
by the tide of bad news; but now I can breathe
again above the flood, and can hear
what anyone has to say, whatever it is.*

BASTARD.
How I have sped among the clergymen
The sums I have collected shall express.
But as I travell'd hither through the land,
I find the people strangely fantasied;
Possess'd with rumours, full of idle dreams.
Not knowing what they fear, but full of fear;
And here's a prophet that I brought with me
From forth the streets of Pomfret, whom I found
With many hundreds treading on his heels;
To whom he sung, in rude harsh-sounding rhymes,
That, ere the next Ascension-day at noon,
Your Highness should deliver up your crown.

*The business I have done amongst the clergymen
will be shown by the sums I have collected.
But as I travelled around the country,
I find that the people are in a strange mood;
they are full of rumours and idle dreams,
they don't know what they're afraid of, but they are
very afraid; and here's a prophet that I brought
with me from out of the streets of Pomfret, whom I
found with many hundreds following him;
and he was singing to them, in coarse vulgar
rhymes, that before noon on the next Ascension
Day your Highness would give up his crown.*

KING JOHN.
Thou idle dreamer, wherefore didst thou so?

You idle dreamer, why were you doing that?

PETER.
Foreknowing that the truth will fall out so.

Because I know that that is what will happen.

KING JOHN.
Hubert, away with him; imprison him;
And on that day at noon whereon he says
I shall yield up my crown let him be hang'd.
Deliver him to safety; and return,

*Hubert, take him away; put him in prison;
and at noon on that day on which he says
I shall give up my crown let him be hanged.
Put him in prison; then come back,*

69

For I must use thee.	*for I need you.*

Exit HUBERT with PETER

O my gentle cousin, Hear'st thou the news abroad, who are arriv'd?	*Oh my gentle cousin,* *have you heard the latest news about who has come?*

BASTARD.

The French, my lord; men's mouths are full of it; Besides, I met Lord Bigot and Lord Salisbury, With eyes as red as new-enkindled fire, And others more, going to seek the grave Of Arthur, whom they say is kill'd to-night On your suggestion.	*The French, my lord; everyone is talking about it;* *besides, I met Lord Bigot and Lord Salisbury,* *with their eyes as red as a newly lit fire,* *and others besides, going to look for the grave* *of Arthur, whom they say was killed tonight* *on your orders.*

KING JOHN.

Gentle kinsman, go And thrust thyself into their companies. I have a way to win their loves again; Bring them before me.	*Sweet kinsman, go* *and join their company.* *I have a way to win back their love;* *bring them to me.*

BASTARD.

I will seek them out.	*I will go and find them.*

KING JOHN.

Nay, but make haste; the better foot before. O, let me have no subject enemies When adverse foreigners affright my towns With dreadful pomp of stout invasion! Be Mercury, set feathers to thy heels, And fly like thought from them to me again.	*No, but hurry; put your best foot forward.* *Oh, don't let me have any native enemies* *while opposing foreigners frighten my towns* *with dreadful displays of harsh invasion!* *Be like Mercury, have winged feet,* *and go from them back to me as quickly as thought.*

BASTARD.

The spirit of the time shall teach me speed.	*The spirit of the time shall show me how to be quick.*

KING JOHN.

Spoke like a sprightful noble gentleman.	*Said like a spirited noble gentleman.*

Exit BASTARD

Go after him; for he perhaps shall need Some messenger betwixt me and the peers; And be thou he.	*Follow him; he may need* *some messenger between me and the peers;* *let that be you.*

MESSENGER.

With all my heart, my liege.	*With all my heart, my lord.*

Exit

KING JOHN.
My mother dead!

Re-enter HUBERT

HUBERT.
My lord, they say five moons were seen to-night;
Four fixed, and the fifth did whirl about
The other four in wondrous motion.

KING JOHN.
Five moons!

HUBERT.
Old men and beldams in the streets
Do prophesy upon it dangerously;
Young Arthur's death is common in their mouths;
And when they talk of him, they shake their heads,
And whisper one another in the ear;
And he that speaks doth gripe the hearer's wrist,
Whilst he that hears makes fearful action
With wrinkled brows, with nods, with rolling eyes.
I saw a smith stand with his hammer, thus,
The whilst his iron did on the anvil cool,
With open mouth swallowing a tailor's news;
Who, with his shears and measure in his hand,
Standing on slippers, which his nimble haste
Had falsely thrust upon contrary feet,
Told of a many thousand warlike French
That were embattailed and rank'd in Kent.
Another lean unwash'd artificer
Cuts off his tale, and talks of Arthur's death.

KING JOHN.
Why seek'st thou to possess me with these fears?
Why urgest thou so oft young Arthur's death?
Thy hand hath murd'red him. I had a mighty cause
To wish him dead, but thou hadst none to kill him.

HUBERT.
No had, my lord! Why, did you not provoke me?

KING JOHN.
It is the curse of kings to be attended
By slaves that take their humours for a warrant
To break within the bloody house of life,
And on the winking of authority
To understand a law; to know the meaning
Of dangerous majesty, when perchance it frowns

My mother dead!

My Lord, they say that five moons were seen tonight; four were still, and the fifth span around the other four in an astonishing way.

Five moons!

Old men and witches in the streets prophesy danger from it; they are all talking about the death of young Arthur; and when they talk of him, they shake their heads, and whisper to each other; and the one who's talking grabs the wrist of his listener, and the listener works his face with frowns, nods, rolling eyes. I saw a smith standing like this with his hammer, whilst his iron cooled on the anvil, open mouthed while he listened to the news of a tailor; he stood with his shears and tape measure in his hand, wearing slippers which in his hurry he had wrongly put on the opposite feet, telling a tale of many thousands of warlike French who were lined up and ready for battle in Kent. Another skinny unwashed workman interrupted him and spoke about Arthur's death.

Why are you trying to worry me like this? Why do you speak so often about the death of young Arthur? It was you who murdered him. I had a great reason for wanting him dead, but you had no reason to kill him.

I had no reason, my lord! Why, did you not order me?

It is the curse of kings that they are surrounded by slaves who think that their moods are orders to attack the bodies of others, and that the wink of a person in authority is the same as a law; they think they know what a dangerous king means, when he might be frowning

71

More upon humour than advis'd respect.	just because of his mood rather than what he wants.
HUBERT. Here is your hand and seal for what I did.	Here are your sealed written orders for what I did.
KING JOHN. O, when the last account 'twixt heaven and earth Is to be made, then shall this hand and seal Witness against us to damnation! How oft the sight of means to do ill deeds Make deeds ill done! Hadst not thou been by, A fellow by the hand of nature mark'd, Quoted and sign'd to do a deed of shame, This murder had not come into my mind; But, taking note of thy abhorr'd aspect, Finding thee fit for bloody villainy, Apt, liable to be employ'd in danger, I faintly broke with thee of Arthur's death; And thou, to be endeared to a king, Made it no conscience to destroy a prince.	Oh, when Judgement Day comes, this writing and this seal will be the evidence which sends me to hell! How often the presence of the means to do wrong encourages one to do wrong! If you hadn't been standing by, a fellow marked out by the hand of nature as one designed to do shameful deeds, I would not have thought of this murder; but, observing your horrible face, seeing that you were suited to bloody villainy, good to be used for dangerous purposes, I faintly mentioned Arthur's death to you; and you, to get the favour of a king, didn't care about killing a prince.
HUBERT. My lord-	My lord—
KING JOHN. Hadst thou but shook thy head or made pause, When I spake darkly what I purposed, Or turn'd an eye of doubt upon my face, As bid me tell my tale in express words, Deep shame had struck me dumb, made me break off, And those thy fears might have wrought fears in me. But thou didst understand me by my signs, And didst in signs again parley with sin; Yea, without stop, didst let thy heart consent, And consequently thy rude hand to act The deed which both our tongues held vile to name. Out of my sight, and never see me more! My nobles leave me; and my state is braved, Even at my gates, with ranks of foreign pow'rs; Nay, in the body of the fleshly land, This kingdom, this confine of blood and breath, Hostility and civil tumult reigns Between my conscience and my cousin's death.	If you had just shaken your head or paused, when I hinted at what I planned, or turned a doubtful eye to my face, telling me to say what I meant outright, deep shame would have struck me down, made me stop, and your worries might have created worries in me. But you understood what I was hinting at, and you hinted that you were ready to do this sin; without a pause you let your heart agree to, and after that your rough hand to do, the deed which both of us dared not speak aloud. Get out of my sight, I don't want to see you again! My nobles have left me; my country is under attack even at my gates with foreign armies; and within my body, this prison of blood and breath, there is a civil war going on between my conscience and the death of my cousin.
HUBERT. Arm you against your other enemies,	Arm yourself against your other enemies,

I'll make a peace between your soul and you.
Young Arthur is alive. This hand of mine
Is yet a maiden and an innocent hand,
Not painted with the crimson spots of blood.
Within this bosom never ent'red yet
The dreadful motion of a murderous thought
And you have slander'd nature in my form,
Which, howsoever rude exteriorly,
Is yet the cover of a fairer mind
Than to be butcher of an innocent child.

KING JOHN.
Doth Arthur live? O, haste thee to the peers,
Throw this report on their incensed rage
And make them tame to their obedience!
Forgive the comment that my passion made
Upon thy feature; for my rage was blind,
And foul imaginary eyes of blood
Presented thee more hideous than thou art.
O, answer not; but to my closet bring
The angry lords with all expedient haste.
I conjure thee but slowly; run more fast.

Exeunt

I will make peace between you and your soul. Young Arthur is alive. This hand of mine is still unsullied and innocent, not covered in blood. My heart has never entertained the dreadful notion of committing murder and you have wronged my nature, for however rough the outside looks it covers a mind that is too good to become the butcher of an innocent child.

Is Arthur alive? Oh, hurry to the peers, confront their anger with this news and make them obedient again! Forgive the comments that I made in anger against your appearance; my anger made me blind, and imagining the bloodshed I thought you had done made you look more hideous than you are. Oh, do not answer me; but bring the angry lords to my room as quick as you can. I am wasting time with my request; run faster than I ask you.

SCENE 3.

England. Before the castle

Enter ARTHUR, on the walls

ARTHUR.
The wall is high, and yet will I leap down.
Good ground, be pitiful and hurt me not!
There's few or none do know me; if they did,
This ship-boy's semblance hath disguis'd me quite.
I am afraid; and yet I'll venture it.
If I get down and do not break my limbs,
I'll find a thousand shifts to get away.
As good to die and go, as die and stay.
[Leaps down]
O me! my uncle's spirit is in these stones.
Heaven take my soul, and England keep my bones!
[Dies]

*The wall is high, but I will still jump down.
Good ground, pity me and don't hurt me!
Hardly anyone knows me; if they did
this sailor boy's disguise makes me unknowable.
I am afraid; and yet I'll risk it.
If I get down and don't break my limbs,
there are a thousand ways for me to escape.
I might just as well die escaping as die staying.
[Leaps down]
Alas! The spirit of my uncle is in the stones.
Heaven receive my soul, and England keep my bones!*

Enter PEMBROKE, SALISBURY, and BIGOT

SALISBURY.
Lords, I will meet him at Saint Edmundsbury;
It is our safety, and we must embrace
This gentle offer of the perilous time.

*Lords, I will meet him at St Edmundsbury;
this will make us safe, and we must accept
this kind offer in this dangerous time.*

PEMBROKE.
Who brought that letter from the Cardinal?

Who brought that letter from the cardinal?

SALISBURY.
The Count Melun, a noble lord of France,
Whose private with me of the Dauphin's love
Is much more general than these lines import.

*Count Melun, a noble lord of France,
who privately told me that the Dauphin's love
is much more comprehensive than is written down.*

BIGOT.
To-morrow morning let us meet him then.

Then let us meet him tomorrow morning.

SALISBURY.
Or rather then set forward; for 'twill be
Two long days' journey, lords, or ere we meet.

*Or rather let us set out then; it will be
a journey of two long days, lords, before we meet.*

Enter the BASTARD

BASTARD.
Once more to-day well met, distemper'd lords!
The King by me requests your presence straight.

*Good to see you once again today, upset lords!
Through me the king asks you to go and see him at once.*

SALISBURY.

The King hath dispossess'd himself of us. We will not line his thin bestained cloak With our pure honours, nor attend the foot That leaves the print of blood where'er it walks. Return and tell him so. We know the worst.	*The King has lost us.* *We will not line his thin stained cloak* *with our honour, nor shall we wait on the foot* *that leaves a bloody footprint wherever it walks.* *Go back and tell him so. We know the worst.*
BASTARD. Whate'er you think, good words, I think, were best.	*Whatever you think, I think that good words are the best.*
SALISBURY. Our griefs, and not our manners, reason now.	*We are being guided by our sorrows, not our manners.*
BASTARD. But there is little reason in your grief; Therefore 'twere reason you had manners now.	*But there is no reason for your sorrow;* *therefore you should be showing some manners now.*
PEMBROKE. Sir, sir, impatience hath his privilege.	*Sir, allowances can be made for anger.*
BASTARD. 'Tis true-to hurt his master, no man else.	*That's true–allowing it to hurt his master, and no one else.*
SALISBURY. This is the prison. What is he lies here?	*This is the prison. Who is this lying here?*
PEMBROKE. O death, made proud with pure and princely beauty! The earth had not a hole to hide this deed.	*Oh death, made so proud by destroying this pure princely beauty!* *There is no grave to hide this action.*
SALISBURY. Murder, as hating what himself hath done, Doth lay it open to urge on revenge.	*It's as if murder hates what he himself has done,* *and leaves it out in the open to encourage revenge.*
BIGOT. Or, when he doom'd this beauty to a grave, Found it too precious-princely for a grave.	*Or, when he sentenced this beauty to a grave,* *decided that it was too precious for the grave.*
SALISBURY. Sir Richard, what think you? Have you beheld, Or have you read or heard, or could you think? Or do you almost think, although you see, That you do see? Could thought, without this object, Form such another? This is the very top, The height, the crest, or crest unto the crest, Of murder's arms; this is the bloodiest shame, The wildest savagery, the vilest stroke, That ever wall-ey'd wrath or staring rage	*Sir Richard, what do you think? Have you seen,* *or have you read or heard, or could you think?* *Or do you almost think, even though you see,* *that you see? Could you possibly have these thoughts* *without this evidence? This is the very top,* *the very highest point of* *murder; this is the bloodiest shame,* *the wildest savagery, the most evil stroke,* *that blind anger or staring rage*

Presented to the tears of soft remorse.

PEMBROKE.
All murders past do stand excus'd in this;
And this, so sole and so unmatchable,
Shall give a holiness, a purity,
To the yet unbegotten sin of times,
And prove a deadly bloodshed but a jest,
Exampled by this heinous spectacle.

BASTARD.
It is a damned and a bloody work;
The graceless action of a heavy hand,
If that it be the work of any hand.

SALISBURY.
If that it be the work of any hand!
We had a kind of light what would ensue.
It is the shameful work of Hubert's hand;
The practice and the purpose of the King;
From whose obedience I forbid my soul
Kneeling before this ruin of sweet life,
And breathing to his breathless excellence
The incense of a vow, a holy vow,
Never to taste the pleasures of the world,
Never to be infected with delight,
Nor conversant with ease and idleness,
Till I have set a glory to this hand
By giving it the worship of revenge.

PEMBROKE. and BIGOT.
Our souls religiously confirm thy words.

Enter HUBERT

HUBERT.
Lords, I am hot with haste in seeking you.
Arthur doth live; the King hath sent for you.

SALISBURY.
O, he is bold, and blushes not at death!
Avaunt, thou hateful villain, get thee gone!

HUBERT.
I am no villain.

SALISBURY.
Must I rob the law?[Drawing his
sword]

ever did to cause tears of soft regret.

*This murder will excuse all the ones in the past;
this one, so unique and inimitable,
will make sins yet to be committed
seem holy and pure,
and make deadly bloodshed just a joke,
when compared to this horrible sight.*

*It is a damnable and bloody deed;
the graceless action of a vicious man,
if it is in fact the work of a man.*

*If it was the work of a man!
We had a hint as to what would happen.
This is the shameful work of Hubert;
the orders come from the King;
I forbid my soul to obey him,
kneeling before this ruin of sweet life,
and in front of his dead excellence
I take a holy vow
that I will never indulge myself in any pleasure,
never enjoy anything,
never know rest or leisure,
until I have given this hand back its glory
by worshipping it with revenge.*

We religiously swear the same.

*Lords, I have rushed as fast as I can to find you.
Arthur is alive; the King has sent for you.*

*Oh, he is bold, he doesn't blush at death!
Get out of here, you horrible villain, begone!*

I am no villain.

Must I steal the executioner's job?

BASTARD.
Your sword is bright, sir; put it up again.

SALISBURY.
Not till I sheathe it in a murderer's skin.

HUBERT.
Stand back, Lord Salisbury, stand back, I say;
By heaven, I think my sword's as sharp as yours.
I would not have you, lord, forget yourself,
Nor tempt the danger of my true defence;
Lest I, by marking of your rage, forget
Your worth, your greatness and nobility.

BIGOT.
Out, dunghill! Dar'st thou brave a nobleman?

HUBERT.
Not for my life; but yet I dare defend
My innocent life against an emperor.

SALISBURY.
Thou art a murderer.

HUBERT.
Do not prove me so.
Yet I am none. Whose tongue soe'er speaks false,
Not truly speaks; who speaks not truly, lies.

PEMBROKE.
Cut him to pieces.

BASTARD.
Keep the peace, I say.

SALISBURY.
Stand by, or I shall gall you, Faulconbridge.

BASTARD.
Thou wert better gall the devil, Salisbury.
If thou but frown on me, or stir thy foot,
Or teach thy hasty spleen to do me shame,
I'll strike thee dead. Put up thy sword betime;
Or I'll so maul you and your toasting-iron
That you shall think the devil is come from hell.

BIGOT.
What wilt thou do, renowned Faulconbridge?
Second a villain and a murderer?

Your sword is bright, sir; put it away.

Not until I put it inside a murderer.

*Stand back, Lord Salisbury, stand back, I say;
by heaven, I think my sword is a sharp as yours.
I don't want you, Lord, to forget yourself,
and to risk taking on my strong skills;
in case I, seeing your rage, forget
your worthiness, your greatness and your nobility.*

Damn you, dunghill! Do you dare to challenge a nobleman?

*Not on my life; but I still would dare to defend
my innocent life against an emperor.*

You are a murderer.

*Do not make me be one.
But I am not one. Whoever says that speaks falsely,
not truthfully; someone who does not speak
truthfully is lying.*

Cut him to pieces.

Keep the peace, I say.

Stand aside, or I will hurt you, Faulconbridge.

*You would be better off hurting the devil,
Salisbury. If you just frown on me, or move
towards me, or try to shame me in your rash anger,
I'll strike you dead. Put away your sword at once;
or I will give you and your toasting iron such a
thrashing
that you'll think the devil has come from hell.*

*What are you going to do, renowned
Faulconbridge? Support a villain and a murderer?*

HUBERT. Lord Bigot, I am none.	*Lord Bigot, I am not one.*
BIGOT. Who kill'd this prince?	*Who killed this prince?*
HUBERT. 'Tis not an hour since I left him well. I honour'd him, I lov'd him, and will weep My date of life out for his sweet life's loss.	*I left him in good health not an hour ago. I respected him, I loved him, and will weep for the rest of my days over the loss of his sweet life.*
SALISBURY. Trust not those cunning waters of his eyes, For villainy is not without such rheum; And he, long traded in it, makes it seem Like rivers of remorse and innocency. Away with me, all you whose souls abhor Th' uncleanly savours of a slaughter-house; For I am stifled with this smell of sin.	*Don't trust those cunning tears of his, for villainy can always summon them up; and he, who has had lots of practice, makes it look as if they are rivers of remorse and innocence. Come away with me, all of you whose souls despise the unclean reek of the slaughterhouse; I am choking on this smell of sin.*
BIGOT. Away toward Bury, to the Dauphin there!	*Let's go to Bury, to the Dauphin!*
PEMBROKE. There tell the King he may inquire us out.	*Tell the King he can find us there.*

Exeunt LORDS

BASTARD. Here's a good world! Knew you of this fair work? Beyond the infinite and boundless reach Of mercy, if thou didst this deed of death, Art thou damn'd, Hubert.	*Here's a fine thing! Did you know about this job? If you did this murder, Hubert, you are damned beyond the infinite reach of mercy.*
HUBERT. Do but hear me, sir.	*Just listen to me, sir.*
BASTARD. Ha! I'll tell thee what: Thou'rt damn'd as black—nay, nothing is so black— Thou art more deep damn'd than Prince Lucifer; There is not yet so ugly a fiend of hell As thou shalt be, if thou didst kill this child.	*Ha! I'll tell you what: you are damned as black—no, there is nothing as black— you are more deeply damned than Prince Lucifer; there isn't a devil in hell as ugly as you will be, if you killed this child.*
HUBERT. Upon my soul—	*I swear on my soul—*
BASTARD. If thou didst but consent	*If you only agreed*

To this most cruel act, do but despair;	to this terrible deed, you should despair;
And if thou want'st a cord, the smallest thread	and if you need a cord, the smallest thread
That ever spider twisted from her womb	that a spider ever span out of her womb
Will serve to strangle thee; a rush will be a beam	will do for strangling you; a reed will make a beam
To hang thee on; or wouldst thou drown thyself,	to hang you from; or if you want to drown yourself,
Put but a little water in a spoon	just put a little water in a spoon
And it shall be as all the ocean,	and it will be like the whole ocean,
Enough to stifle such a villain up.	enough to suffocate such a villain.
I do suspect thee very grievously.	I have very strong suspicions of you.

HUBERT.

If I in act, consent, or sin of thought,	If by action, agreement, or sinful thinking,
Be guilty of the stealing that sweet breath	I was guilty of stealing away that sweet breath
Which was embounded in this beauteous clay,	which was contained within this beautiful body,
Let hell want pains enough to torture me!	may hell run out of tortures to use on me!
I left him well.	I left him healthy.

BASTARD.

Go, bear him in thine arms.	Go, carry him in your arms.
I am amaz'd, methinks, and lose my way	I am bewildered, I think, and I have lost my way
Among the thorns and dangers of this world.	amongst the thorns and dangers of this world.
How easy dost thou take all England up!	How easy it is for you to pick up the whole of
From forth this morsel of dead royalty	England in the person of this dead royal body!
The life, the right, and truth of all this realm	The life, rights and truth of this whole country
Is fled to heaven; and England now is left	have gone to heaven; and now England is left
To tug and scamble, and to part by th' teeth	to push and shove, and to tear apart in their teeth
The unowed interest of proud-swelling state.	the unruled powers of the great nation.
Now for the bare-pick'd bone of majesty	Now the dog of war raises his angry hackles
Doth dogged war bristle his angry crest	to fight for the stripped bones of majesty
And snarleth in the gentle eyes of peace;	and snarls in the gentle face of peace;
Now powers from home and discontents at home	now forces from abroad and civil discontent
Meet in one line; and vast confusion waits,	come together as one; great chaos awaits,
As doth a raven on a sick-fall'n beast,	like a raven hovering over a sick man,
The imminent decay of wrested pomp.	following the general collapse when the throne is
Now happy he whose cloak and cincture can	stolen. It will be a lucky man who manages
Hold out this tempest. Bear away that child,	to ride out the storm. Carry away that child,
And follow me with speed. I'll to the King;	and follow me quickly. I'll go to the king;
A thousand businesses are brief in hand,	there are a thousand things which need seeing to,
And heaven itself doth frown upon the land.	and heaven is frowning over the country.

Exeunt

Act V

SCENE 1.

England. KING JOHN'S palace

Enter KING JOHN, PANDULPH, and attendants

KING JOHN.
Thus have I yielded up into your hand
The circle of my glory.

So I have surrendered my crown into your hand.

PANDULPH.
[Gives back the crown]Take again
From this my hand, as holding of the Pope,
Your sovereign greatness and authority.

Take it back again from my hand, as a representative of the Pope, take back your royal greatness and authority.

KING JOHN.
Now keep your holy word; go meet the French;
And from his Holiness use all your power
To stop their marches fore we are inflam'd.
Our discontented counties do revolt;
Our people quarrel with obedience,
Swearing allegiance and the love of soul
To stranger blood, to foreign royalty.
This inundation of mistemp'red humour
Rests by you only to be qualified.
Then pause not; for the present time's so sick
That present med'cine must be minist'red
Or overthrow incurable ensues.

Now keep your holy word; go and meet French; and use all power you have from the Pope to stop their advances before we are overcome. Our discontented counties are rebelling; our people are refusing to obey, swearing allegiance and pledging their souls to foreign blood and royalty. This flood of disordered moods can only be abated by you. So don't wait; the time is so sick that it must be given medicine at once or it will be followed by incurable collapse.

PANDULPH.
It was my breath that blew this tempest up,
Upon your stubborn usage of the Pope;
But since you are a gentle convertite,
My tongue shall hush again this storm of war
And make fair weather in your blust'ring land.
On this Ascension-day, remember well,
Upon your oath of service to the Pope,
Go I to make the French lay down their arms.

It was I who started this storm, due to your insult to the Pope, but since you have sweetly reconverted, I shall calm down this storm of war and bring fair weather to your windy land. Remember on every Ascension day like this your oath of service to the Pope, and I will go and make the French retreat.

Exit

KING JOHN.
Is this Ascension-day? Did not the prophet
Say that before Ascension-day at noon
My crown I should give off? Even so I have.
I did suppose it should be on constraint;
But, heaven be thank'd, it is but voluntary.

Is this Ascension Day? Didn't the prophet say that before Ascension day at noon I should give up my crown? Well I have. I imagined that I would be forced to; but, thank heaven, it was only voluntary.

Enter the BASTARD

81

BASTARD.
All Kent hath yielded; nothing there holds out
But Dover Castle. London hath receiv'd,
Like a kind host, the Dauphin and his powers.
Your nobles will not hear you, but are gone
To offer service to your enemy;
And wild amazement hurries up and down
The little number of your doubtful friends.

KING JOHN.
Would not my lords return to me again
After they heard young Arthur was alive?

BASTARD.
They found him dead, and cast into the streets,
An empty casket, where the jewel of life
By some damn'd hand was robbed and ta'en away.

KING JOHN.
That villain Hubert told me he did live.

BASTARD.
So, on my soul, he did, for aught he knew.
But wherefore do you droop? Why look you sad?
Be great in act, as you have been in thought;
Let not the world see fear and sad distrust
Govern the motion of a kingly eye.
Be stirring as the time; be fire with fire;
Threaten the threat'ner, and outface the brow
Of bragging horror; so shall inferior eyes,
That borrow their behaviours from the great,
Grow great by your example and put on
The dauntless spirit of resolution.
Away, and glister like the god of war
When he intendeth to become the field;
Show boldness and aspiring confidence.
What, shall they seek the lion in his den,
And fright him there, and make him tremble there?
O, let it not be said! Forage, and run
To meet displeasure farther from the doors
And grapple with him ere he come so nigh.

KING JOHN.
The legate of the Pope hath been with me,
And I have made a happy peace with him;
And he hath promis'd to dismiss the powers
Led by the Dauphin.

BASTARD.

All of Kent has surrendered; only Dover Castle has resisted. London has welcomed, like a kind host, the Dauphin and his forces. The nobles will not listen to you, they have gone to offer their services to your enemy; and wild confusion is buzzing around the small number of your fearful friends.

Wouldn't my Lords come back to me after they heard young Arthur was alive?

They found him dead, and thrown into the street, an empty casket from which some damnable hand had robbed and taken away the jewel of life.

That villain Hubert told me he was alive.

I swear he thought that that was true. But why are you drooping? Why do you look so sad? Be as great in action as you have been in thought; don't let the world see fear and doubt ruling the eye of the King. Be as active as the situation; fight fire with fire; threaten those who threaten you, and stare down arrogant terror; so inferior people, who copy the greatness of their betters, will become great through your example and gather up dare dauntless resolve. Go, and shine like the God of War when he intends to join the battle; showed bravery and great confidence. What, shall they look for the lion in his den, and frighten him there, make him tremble? Oh, don't say that! Go out, and run to meet the opposition farther from the doors and fight with him before he gets so close.

The Pope's representative has been here, and I have arranged a happy peace with him; he has promised to make the Dauphin withdraw his forces.

O inglorious league!
Shall we, upon the footing of our land,
Send fair-play orders, and make compromise,
Insinuation, parley, and base truce,
To arms invasive? Shall a beardless boy,
A cock'red silken wanton, brave our fields
And flesh his spirit in a warlike soil,
Mocking the air with colours idly spread,
And find no check? Let us, my liege, to arms.
Perchance the Cardinal cannot make your peace;
Or, if he do, let it at least be said
They saw we had a purpose of defence.

What a shameful alliance!
Shall we, standing in our own country,
bow down and ask for compromise,
ingratiate ourselves, speak sweetly and make
shameful truces with invaders? Shall a beardless
boy, a spoilt silky brat, show off in our fields
and learn to fight on our warlike soil,
mocking the air with his flags carelessly waving,
and not be stopped? Let us take up arms, my lord.
Perhaps the cardinal might be able to make peace;
or, if he does, let it be said that at least
they saw that we could have defended ourselves.

KING JOHN.
Have thou the ordering of this present time.

You have command in this situation.

BASTARD.
Away, then, with good courage!
Yet, I know
Our party may well meet a prouder foe.

Come on then, and be confident!
but I know that we could easily beat a better
enemy.

Exeunt

SCENE 2.

England. The DAUPHIN'S camp at Saint Edmundsbury

Enter, in arms, LEWIS, SALISBURY, MELUN, PEMBROKE, BIGOT, and soldiers

LEWIS.
My Lord Melun, let this be copied out
And keep it safe for our remembrance;
Return the precedent to these lords again,
That, having our fair order written down,
Both they and we, perusing o'er these notes,
May know wherefore we took the sacrament,
And keep our faiths firm and inviolable.

SALISBURY.
Upon our sides it never shall be broken.
And, noble Dauphin, albeit we swear
A voluntary zeal and an unurg'd faith
To your proceedings; yet, believe me, Prince,
I am not glad that such a sore of time
Should seek a plaster by contemn'd revolt,
And heal the inveterate canker of one wound
By making many. O, it grieves my soul
That I must draw this metal from my side
To be a widow-maker! O, and there
Where honourable rescue and defence
Cries out upon the name of Salisbury!
But such is the infection of the time
That, for the health and physic of our right,
We cannot deal but with the very hand
Of stern injustice and confused wrong.
And is't not pity, O my grieved friends!
That we, the sons and children of this isle,
Were born to see so sad an hour as this;
Wherein we step after a stranger-march
Upon her gentle bosom, and fill up
Her enemies' ranks—I must withdraw and weep
Upon the spot of this enforced cause—
To grace the gentry of a land remote
And follow unacquainted colours here?
What, here? O nation, that thou couldst remove!
That Neptune's arms, who clippeth thee about,
Would bear thee from the knowledge of thyself
And grapple thee unto a pagan shore,
Where these two Christian armies might combine
The blood of malice in a vein of league,
And not to spend it so unneighbourly!

*My Lord Melun, copy this out
and keep it safe as a reminder;
take the original back to these lords,
so that, having our fair order written down,
both we and they, when we look over these notes,
will know why we made this holy oath,
and keep our faith firm and unbreakable.*

*Nobody on this side shall ever break it.
And, noble Dauphin, although we swear
voluntarily and give you our consent to your
proceedings without force; still believe me, prince,
I'm not happy that this time is so wounded
that it has to be cured with a horrible revolt,
and that we have to heal the disease of one wound
by making many. And it grieves my soul,
that I must unsheathe my sword
and make widows with it! In the place where
people appeal to Salisbury for
honourable rescue and defence!
But things are so wrong
that for the healthy cure of the time
we can only deal with the one who has dealt
out harsh injustice and confused wrongs.
Isn't it shameful, my sorrowing friends,
that we, the sons and children of this island,
were born to see such a sad time is this;
in which we follow a foreigner, march
across her sweet lands, and reinforce
the ranks of her enemies—I must stand aside and
weep at the stain of this enforced action—
to adorn the nobility of a remote country,
and follow their unfamiliar banners here?
What, here? Oh nation, if only you could move!
If only Neptune, whose ocean surrounds you,
could carry you away from knowledge of yourself—
handicap you—to a pagan shore,
where these two Christian armies could join
their harmful power together in alliance,
and not spend it on such unneighbourly activities!*

LEWIS.
A noble temper dost thou show in this;
And great affections wrestling in thy bosom
Doth make an earthquake of nobility.
O, what a noble combat hast thou fought
Between compulsion and a brave respect!
Let me wipe off this honourable dew
That silverly doth progress on thy cheeks.
My heart hath melted at a lady's tears,
Being an ordinary inundation;
But this effusion of such manly drops,
This show'r, blown up by tempest of the soul,
Startles mine eyes and makes me more amaz'd
Than had I seen the vaulty top of heaven
Figur'd quite o'er with burning meteors.
Lift up thy brow, renowned Salisbury,
And with a great heart heave away this storm;
Commend these waters to those baby eyes
That never saw the giant world enrag'd,
Nor met with fortune other than at feasts,
Full of warm blood, of mirth, of gossiping.
Come, come; for thou shalt thrust thy hand as deep
Into the purse of rich prosperity
As Lewis himself. So, nobles, shall you all,
That knit your sinews to the strength of mine.

Enter PANDULPH

And even there, methinks, an angel spake:
Look where the holy legate comes apace,
To give us warrant from the hand of heaven
And on our actions set the name of right
With holy breath.

PANDULPH.
Hail, noble prince of France!
The next is this: King John hath reconcil'd
Himself to Rome; his spirit is come in,
That so stood out against the holy Church,
The great metropolis and see of Rome.
Therefore thy threat'ning colours now wind up
And tame the savage spirit of wild war,
That, like a lion fostered up at hand,
It may lie gently at the foot of peace
And be no further harmful than in show.

LEWIS.
Your Grace shall pardon me, I will not back:
I am too high-born to be propertied,

*You show a noble spirit in saying this;
and the great loyalties wrestling in your heart
make an earthquake of nobility.
Oh, what a noble combat you have fought
between what you were compelled to do and what
was right! Let me wipe off this honourable dew,
that runs in silver streams down your cheeks:
my heart has been melted by a lady's tears,
just an ordinary flood;
but this stream of such manly drops,
this shower, blown up by the storm in your soul,
amazes me, more so than
if I had seen the heights of heaven
absolutely covered with fiery meteors. Look up,
renowned Salisbury,
and with a great heart push this storm away:
leave these tears to the eyes of babies
who never saw the whole world in conflict,
and never met fortune except in good
circumstances, with warm blood, happiness and
gossiping. Come, come; you shall gain as much
from this action as
I will myself: so, nobles, shall you all,
everyone who joins forces with me.*

[Enter Pandulph]

*And just then, I think, an angel spoke:
look, here comes the Pope's representative
to give us permission from the agent of heaven,
to seal our actions as being right
with holy breath.*

*Greetings, noble Prince of France!
This is the news: King John has reconciled
himself with Rome; the spirit that so rebelled
against the holy Church, the great city and
seat of Rome, has come back.
So take down your military flags
and calm the savage spirit of wild war,
so that, like a lion raised by hand,
it may lie gently at the foot of peace
and only look dangerous.*

*Your Grace must excuse me, I will not retreat:
I am too noble to the used as a tool,*

85

To be a secondary at control,
Or useful serving-man and instrument
To any sovereign state throughout the world.
Your breath first kindled the dead coal of wars
Between this chastis'd kingdom and myself
And brought in matter that should feed this fire;
And now 'tis far too huge to be blown out
With that same weak wind which enkindled it.
You taught me how to know the face of right,
Acquainted me with interest to this land,
Yea, thrust this enterprise into my heart;
And come ye now to tell me John hath made
His peace with Rome? What is that peace to me?
I, by the honour of my marriage-bed,
After young Arthur, claim this land for mine;
And, now it is half-conquer'd, must I back
Because that John hath made his peace with Rome?
Am I Rome's slave? What penny hath Rome borne,
What men provided, what munition sent,
To underprop this action? Is 't not I
That undergo this charge? Who else but I,
And such as to my claim are liable,
Sweat in this business and maintain this war?
Have I not heard these islanders shout out
'Vive le roi!' as I have bank'd their towns?
Have I not here the best cards for the game
To will this easy match, play'd for a crown?
And shall I now give o'er the yielded set?
No, no, on my soul, it never shall be said.

PANDULPH.
You look but on the outside of this work.

LEWIS.
Outside or inside, I will not return
Till my attempt so much be glorified
As to my ample hope was promised
Before I drew this gallant head of war,
And cull'd these fiery spirits from the world
To outlook conquest, and to win renown
Even in the jaws of danger and of death.
 [Trumpet sounds]
What lusty trumpet thus doth summon us?

Enter the BASTARD, attended

BASTARD.
According to the fair play of the world,
Let me have audience: I am sent to speak.

---

to be under the control of another,
to be a useful serving man and instrument
of any royal state throughout the world.
It was your words which first fanned the flames
of war between this punished kingdom and myself,
and gave reasons for it to carry on;
it's now far too big to be blown out
by the same weak breath which started it.
You taught me how to know what was right,
and showed me why I should conquer this land,
indeed, you were the one who encouraged me;
and now you come to tell me that John has made
his peace with Rome? What does that peace matter
to me? Through the honour of my marriage I am
the next in line to claim this land after young
Arthur; and, now it is half won, must I retreat
because John has made his peace with Rome?
Am I the slave of Rome? What money has Rome
spent, what men has it given, what arms has it sent,
to support this action? Aren't I the one
who's paid for all this? Who else but me,
and those who are subject to my claim,
have sweated in this business and supported this
war? Haven't I heard these islanders shouting out
"Long live the King!" as I won over their towns?
Don't I hold all the best cards in the game
to win this easy victory for a crown?
Show I now hand over the whole set?
No, no, I swear on my soul, I shall never do it.

You only understand the outside of this business.

Outside or inside, I will not go back
until my attempt is glorified
with the great success I hoped for
before I raised this brave army,
and chose these fiery spirits
to face down conquerors, and to win fame
even in the jaws of danger and death.
[Trumpet sounds]
what loud trumpet is this calling us?

According to the general rules of the world,
listen to me: I have been sent to speak.

My holy lord of Milan, from the King
I come, to learn how you have dealt for him;
And, as you answer, I do know the scope
And warrant limited unto my tongue.

PANDULPH.
The Dauphin is too wilful-opposite,
And will not temporize with my entreaties;
He flatly says he'll not lay down his arms.

BASTARD.
By all the blood that ever fury breath'd,
The youth says well. Now hear our English King;
For thus his royalty doth speak in me.
He is prepar'd, and reason too he should.
This apish and unmannerly approach,
This harness'd masque and unadvised revel
This unhair'd sauciness and boyish troops,
The King doth smile at; and is well prepar'd
To whip this dwarfish war, these pigmy arms,
From out the circle of his territories.
That hand which had the strength, even at your door.
To cudgel you and make you take the hatch,
To dive like buckets in concealed wells,
To crouch in litter of your stable planks,
To lie like pawns lock'd up in chests and trunks,
To hug with swine, to seek sweet safety out
In vaults and prisons, and to thrill and shake
Even at the crying of your nation's crow,
Thinking this voice an armed Englishman—
Shall that victorious hand be feebled here
That in your chambers gave you chastisement?
No. Know the gallant monarch is in arms
And like an eagle o'er his aery tow'rs
To souse annoyance that comes near his nest.
And you degenerate, you ingrate revolts,
You bloody Neroes, ripping up the womb
Of your dear mother England, blush for shame;
For your own ladies and pale-visag'd maids,
Like Amazons, come tripping after drums,
Their thimbles into armed gauntlets change,
Their needles to lances, and their gentle hearts
To fierce and bloody inclination.

LEWIS.
There end thy brave, and turn thy face in peace;
We grant thou canst outscold us. Fare thee well;
We hold our time too precious to be spent

My holy Lord of Milan, I have come from the King, to find out what you have done for him; what I say depends upon your answer.

The Dauphin is too wilful and contrary, and will not agree to my pleas; he outright says that he will not retreat.

By all the blood that fury ever breathed, the young man speaks well. Now hear our English king, for this is what he royally says through me: he is ready, and he has reason to be— this apelike rude approach, this show in armour and foolish revelling, this beardless cheek with his boyish troops, the king smiles at; and he is well-prepared to beat this little war, this pigmy army, right out of his lands— the hand that had the strength to come up to your door, to beat you and make you bolt it, to make you dive like buckets into hidden wells, to crouch in the straw of your stables, to lie like pawns locked up in chests and trunks, to hug your pigs, to look for sweet safety in vaults and prisons, and to shiver and shake even when you heard your national bird crowing, thinking that the noise was an armed Englishman; will that victorious hand be held back here, who beat you in your own rooms? No: the brave king is prepared like an eagle hovering over his high nests, ready to swoop on any annoyance which comes near. And you degenerate ungrateful rebels, you bloody Neros, ripping up the womb of your dear mother England, blush for shame: for your own ladies and pale faced girls come tripping after the drums like Amazons, with their thimbles changed into armed gloves, their needles into lances, and their gentle hearts changed to fierce and bloody thoughts.

Stop your bravado there, and turn away in peace; we admit that you can outquarrel us. Farewell; our time is too precious to us to be wasted

87

With such a brabbler. | on such a brawler.

PANDULPH.
Give me leave to speak. | Give me permission to speak.

BASTARD.
No, I will speak. | No, I will speak.

LEWIS.
We will attend to neither.
Strike up the drums; and let the tongue of war,
Plead for our interest and our being here.

*I will listen to neither of you.
Strike up the drums; let the voice of war
speak for our interests and our rights.*

BASTARD.
Indeed, your drums, being beaten, will cry out;
And so shall you, being beaten. Do but start
And echo with the clamour of thy drum,
And even at hand a drum is ready brac'd
That shall reverberate all as loud as thine:
Sound but another, and another shall,
As loud as thine, rattle the welkin's ear
And mock the deep-mouth'd thunder; for at hand—
Not trusting to this halting legate here,
Whom he hath us'd rather for sport than need—
Is warlike John; and in his forehead sits
A bare-ribb'd death, whose office is this day
To feast upon whole thousands of the French.

*Indeed, your drums, being beaten, will cry out;
and so will you, when you're beaten. Just start
making a noise with your drums,
close by there is a drum ready prepared
to make a noise just as loud as yours:
sound another and you will be matched with one
just as loud as yours which will shake the skies
and imitate the growling thunder; for close by—
not trusting this weak delegate here,
whom he has used as a joke rather than because he
needed him—
is warlike John; and along with him there is
the skeleton of death, whose work this day
is to gobble up many thousands of Frenchmen.*

LEWIS.
Strike up our drums to find this danger out. | *Beat our drums to reveal this danger.*

BASTARD.
And thou shalt find it, Dauphin, do not doubt. | *And don't doubt that you will find it, Dauphin.*

Exeunt

SCENE 3.

England. The field of battle

Alarums. Enter KING JOHN and HUBERT

KING JOHN.
How goes the day with us? O, tell me, Hubert.

HUBERT.
Badly, I fear. How fares your Majesty?

KING JOHN.
This fever that hath troubled me so long
Lies heavy on me. O, my heart is sick!

Enter a MESSENGER

MESSENGER.
My lord, your valiant kinsman, Faulconbridge,
Desires your Majesty to leave the field
And send him word by me which way you go.

KING JOHN.
Tell him, toward Swinstead, to the abbey there.

MESSENGER.
Be of good comfort; for the great supply
That was expected by the Dauphin here
Are wreck'd three nights ago on Goodwin Sands;
This news was brought to Richard but even now.
The French fight coldly, and retire themselves.

KING JOHN.
Ay me, this tyrant fever burns me up
And will not let me welcome this good news.
Set on toward Swinstead; to my litter straight;
Weakness possesseth me, and I am faint.

Exeunt

How is the battle going with us? Oh, tell me, Hubert.

Badly, I'm afraid. How is your Majesty doing?

This fever that has bothered me for so long it is very strong. Oh, I am sick to my heart!

My lord, your brave kinsman, Faulconbridge, request that your Majesty leaves the battlefield and send him a message via me as to where you go.

Tell him I'll go towards Swinstead, to the abbey there.

Be consoled; for the great force that the Dauphin was expecting here was wrecked three nights ago on Goodwin Sands; Richard has just received the news. The French are fighting defensively, and retreating.

Alas, this overbearing fever burns me up and won't let me celebrate this good news. Go towards Swinstead; put me on my litter; weakness overcomes me, and I am faint.

SCENE 4.

England. Another part of the battlefield

Enter SALISBURY, PEMBROKE, and BIGOT

SALISBURY.
I did not think the King so stor'd with friends. | *I didn't think that the King had such support.*

PEMBROKE.
Up once again; put spirit in the French; | *Back into battle; put courage into the French;*
If they miscarry, we miscarry too. | *if they fail, we fail too.*

SALISBURY.
That misbegotten devil, Faulconbridge, | *That devilish bastard Faulconbridge,*
In spite of spite, alone upholds the day. | *against all the odds, is keeping his side afloat.*

PEMBROKE.
They say King John, sore sick, hath left the field. | *They say that King John has left the battlefield, very sick.*

Enter MELUN, wounded

MELUN.
Lead me to the revolts of England here. | *Take me to the English rebels.*

SALISBURY.
When we were happy we had other names. | *When things were going well we were called differently.*

PEMBROKE.
It is the Count Melun. | *It is the Count Melun.*

SALISBURY.
Wounded to death. | *Fatally wounded.*

MELUN.
Fly, noble English, you are bought and sold; | *Flee, noble Englishmen, you have been sold out;*
Unthread the rude eye of rebellion, | *unpick your rude rebellion,*
And welcome home again discarded faith. | *and resume the loyalty you had before.*
Seek out King John, and fall before his feet; | *Look for King John and fall at his feet;*
For if the French be lords of this loud day, | *for if the French win this great battle,*
He means to recompense the pains you take | *we intend to pay you back for your efforts*
By cutting off your heads. Thus hath he sworn, | *by cutting off your heads. This is what the King of*
And I with him, and many moe with me, | *France has sworn, along with me and many others,*
Upon the altar at Saint Edmundsbury; | *on the altar at St Edmundsbury;*
Even on that altar where we swore to you | *on the same altar where we swore to you*
Dear amity and everlasting love. | *dear friendship and everlasting love.*

SALISBURY.
May this be possible? May this be true? | *Can this be possible? Can it be true?*

MELUN.
Have I not hideous death within my view,
Retaining but a quantity of life,
Which bleeds away even as a form of wax
Resolveth from his figure 'gainst the fire?
What in the world should make me now deceive,
Since I must lose the use of all deceit?
Why should I then be false, since it is true
That I must die here, and live hence by truth?
I say again, if Lewis do will the day,
He is forsworn if e'er those eyes of yours
Behold another day break in the east;
But even this night, whose black contagious breath
Already smokes about the burning crest
Of the old, feeble, and day-wearied sun,
Even this ill night, your breathing shall expire,
Paying the fine of rated treachery
Even with a treacherous fine of all your lives.
If Lewis by your assistance win the day.
Commend me to one Hubert, with your King;
The love of him-and this respect besides,
For that my grandsire was an Englishman-
Awakes my conscience to confess all this.
In lieu whereof, I pray you, bear me hence
From forth the noise and rumour of the field,
Where I may think the remnant of my thoughts
In peace, and part this body and my soul
With contemplation and devout desires.

*Do I not have horrible death within my sight,
only just hanging on to life
which is bleeding away, like a waxwork
dissolving in the fire?
What in the world would make me now lie to you,
when I will soon be unable to lie at all?
Why should I be false, since it is true
that I must die here and go and live where there is
only truth? I say again, if Louis wins the battle,
he has promised that those eyes of yours
will never see another sunrise:
this very night, his black poisonous breath
is already curling around the burning top
of the old, feeble sun, worn out by the day,
on this evil night, you shall cease to breathe,
paying the price for what is seen as treachery
with the terrible fine of all your lives,
if Louis wins the battle with your help.
Give my greetings to a man called Hubert who's
with your king: my love for him, and also the fact
that my grandfather was an Englishman,
provokes my conscience to say all this.
In payment for that, I pray you, carry me away
from the noise and clamour of the battlefield,
where I can think what's left of my thoughts
in peace, and separate my body from my soul
with contemplation and prayer.*

SALISBURY.
We do believe thee; and beshrew my soul
But I do love the favour and the form
Of this most fair occasion, by the which
We will untread the steps of damned flight,
And like a bated and retired flood,
Leaving our rankness and irregular course,
Stoop low within those bounds we have o'erlook'd,
And calmly run on in obedience
Even to our ocean, to great King John.
My arm shall give thee help to bear thee hence;
For I do see the cruel pangs of death
Right in thine eye. Away, my friends! New flight,
And happy newness, that intends old right.

*We believe you; and curse me
if I don't love the way
things are turning out, which means
we can undo our cursed retreat,
and like a flood which has abated
we can leave our foulness and unusual course,
bow down within the frontiers we overcame,
and run obediently and calmly on
to our ocean, our great King John.
I shall help to carry you away from here;
for I can see the cruel agony of death
right in your eyes. Let's go, my friends! A new
escape; a happy newness, taking us back to our old
position!*

Exeunt, leading off MELUN

SCENE 5.

England. The French camp

Enter LEWIS and his train

LEWIS.
The sun of heaven, methought, was loath to set,
But stay'd and made the western welkin blush,
When English measure backward their own ground
In faint retire. O, bravely came we off,
When with a volley of our needless shot,
After such bloody toil, we bid good night;
And wound our tott'ring colours clearly up,
Last in the field and almost lords of it!

It seemed to me that the sun in heaven didn't want to set, but stayed to make the western sky blush, when the English meekly retreated. Oh, we succeeded bravely, when we said good night to them after such bloodthirsty work with a needless volley of artillery; we rolled up our waving banners, the last ones on the battlefield and almost the lords of it!

Enter a MESSENGER

MESSENGER.
Where is my prince, the Dauphin?

Where is my Prince, the Dauphin?

LEWIS.
Here; what news?

Here; what's the news?

MESSENGER.
The Count Melun is slain; the English lords
By his persuasion are again fall'n off,
And your supply, which you have wish'd so long,
Are cast away and sunk on Goodwin Sands.

Count Melun has been killed; the English lords have retreated again on his advice, and your forces, which you have been waiting for so long, are shipwrecked and sunk on Goodwin Sands.

LEWIS.
Ah, foul shrewd news! Beshrew thy very heart!
I did not think to be so sad to-night
As this hath made me. Who was he that said
King John did fly an hour or two before
The stumbling night did part our weary pow'rs?

Such foul and damned news! Damn your very heart! I didn't think that I would be so sad tonight as this has made me. Who said that King John escaped an hour or two before the obscuring night parted our tired armies?

MESSENGER.
Whoever spoke it, it is true, my lord.

Whoever said it, it is true, my lord.

LEWIS.
Keep good quarter and good care to-night;
The day shall not be up so soon as I
To try the fair adventure of to-morrow.

Keep a careful guard tonight; the sun will not have risen before I start my plans for tomorrow.

Exeunt

SCENE 6.

An open place wear Swinstead Abbey

Enter the BASTARD and HUBERT, severally

HUBERT.
Who's there? Speak, ho! speak quickly, or I shoot.

Who's there? Speak out! Speak quickly, or I'll shoot.

BASTARD.
A friend. What art thou?

A friend. Who are you?

HUBERT.
Of the part of England.

On the side of England.

BASTARD.
Whither dost thou go?

Where are you going?

HUBERT.
What's that to thee? Why may I not demand
Of thine affairs as well as thou of mine?

What business is that of yours? Why can't I ask what you're doing the same way you're asking me?

BASTARD.
Hubert, I think.

You are Hubert, I think.

HUBERT.
Thou hast a perfect thought.
I will upon all hazards well believe
Thou art my friend that know'st my tongue so well.
Who art thou?

You think right. I would bet anything that you must be my friend if you know my voice so well. Who are you?

BASTARD.
Who thou wilt. And if thou please,
Thou mayst befriend me so much as to think
I come one way of the Plantagenets.

Whoever you want me to be. And if you want, you can be friendly enough to me to think that on one side I am descended from the Plantagenets.

HUBERT.
Unkind remembrance! thou and eyeless night
Have done me shame. Brave soldier, pardon me
That any accent breaking from thy tongue
Should scape the true acquaintance of mine ear.

Useless memory! You and the blind night have embarrassed me. Brave soldier, excuse me for not recognising your voice.

BASTARD.
Come, come; sans compliment, what news abroad?

Come, come; forget the formalities, what's the news?

HUBERT.
Why, here walk I in the black brow of night
To find you out.

Why, I have been walking through the dark night looking for you.

93

BASTARD.
Brief, then; and what's the news?

You've done it, then; and what's the news?

HUBERT.
O, my sweet sir, news fitting to the night,
Black, fearful, comfortless, and horrible.

Oh, my sweet sir, news which is suitable for the night, Black, fearful, comfortless and horrible.

BASTARD.
Show me the very wound of this ill news;
I am no woman, I'll not swoon at it.

Tell me the results of this bad news; I'm not a woman, it won't make me faint.

HUBERT.
The King, I fear, is poison'd by a monk;
I left him almost speechless and broke out
To acquaint you with this evil, that you might
The better arm you to the sudden time
Than if you had at leisure known of this.

I'm afraid that the King has been poisoned by a monk; I left him almost unable to speak and escaped to tell you of this evil, so that you might be more prepared to deal with the emergency than if you had found out later.

BASTARD.
How did he take it; who did taste to him?

Why did he eat it; who was his food taster?

HUBERT.
A monk, I tell you; a resolved villain,
Whose bowels suddenly burst out. The King
Yet speaks, and peradventure may recover.

A monk, I'm telling you; a complete villain, whose bowels suddenly exploded. The King is still speaking, and there's a chance he may recover.

BASTARD.
Who didst thou leave to tend his Majesty?

Who did you leave looking after his Majesty?

HUBERT.
Why, know you not? The lords are all come back,
And brought Prince Henry in their company;
At whose request the King hath pardon'd them,
And they are all about his Majesty.

Why, haven't you heard? The lords have all come back, and brought Prince Henry with them; at his request the King has pardoned them, and they are all with his Majesty.

BASTARD.
Withhold thine indignation, mighty heaven,
And tempt us not to bear above our power!
I'll tell thee, Hubert, half my power this night,
Passing these flats, are taken by the tide-

These Lincoln Washes have devoured them;
Myself, well-mounted, hardly have escap'd.
Away, before! conduct me to the King;
I doubt he will be dead or ere I come.

Exeunt

SCENE 7.

The orchard at Swinstead Abbey

Enter PRINCE HENRY, SALISBURY, and BIGOT

PRINCE HENRY.
It is too late; the life of all his blood
Is touch'd corruptibly, and his pure brain.
Which some suppose the soul's frail dwelling-house,
Doth by the idle comments that it makes
Foretell the ending of mortality.

It's too late; all of his lifeblood has been corrupted, as well as his pure brain, which some imagine is where the soul lives, which shows by the strange comments that it makes that it is about to die.

Enter PEMBROKE

PEMBROKE.
His Highness yet doth speak, and holds belief
That, being brought into the open air,
It would allay the burning quality
Of that fell poison which assaileth him.

His Highness is still speaking, and believes that if he was brought into the open air it would soften the burning of the evil poison which is attacking him.

PRINCE HENRY.
Let him be brought into the orchard here.
Doth he still rage?

Bring him out into the orchard here. Is he still raving?

Exit BIGOT

PEMBROKE.
He is more patient
Than when you left him; even now he sung.

He's calmer than when you left him; just now he sung.

PRINCE HENRY.
O vanity of sickness! Fierce extremes
In their continuance will not feel themselves.
Death, having prey'd upon the outward parts,
Leaves them invisible, and his siege is now
Against the mind, the which he pricks and wounds
With many legions of strange fantasies,
Which, in their throng and press to that last hold,
Confound themselves. 'Tis strange that death should sing.
I am the cygnet to this pale faint swan
Who chants a doleful hymn to his own death,
And from the organ-pipe of frailty sings
His soul and body to their lasting rest.

The deceitfulness of sickness! When you reach these outer limits you do not know you're there. Death, having triumphed over the outer shell, disappears from it and he now attacks the mind, which he pricks and wounds with great throngs of strange fantasies, which, as they press forward on that last defence, destroy themselves. It's strange that death should sing. I am the cygnet of this pale faint swan who sings a sad hymn for his own death and with his weak voice sings his soul and body to their eternal rest.

SALISBURY.
Be of good comfort, Prince; for you are born

Console yourself, Prince; for you were born

To set a form upon that indigest
Which he hath left so shapeless and so rude.

to bring order to this chaos
which he has left so formless and rough.

Re-enter BIGOT and attendants, who bring in KING JOHN in a chair

KING JOHN.
Ay, marry, now my soul hath elbow-room;
It would not out at windows nor at doors.
There is so hot a summer in my bosom
That all my bowels crumble up to dust.
I am a scribbled form drawn with a pen
Upon a parchment, and against this fire
Do I shrink up.

Ah, that's better, now my soul has elbow room;
it can't get out of windows or doors.
There is such a hot summer in my heart
that my bowels crumble into dust.
I am a scribbled picture drawn with a pen
on a parchment, and this fire
shrivels me up.

PRINCE HENRY.
How fares your Majesty?

How is your Majesty?

KING JOHN.
Poison'd-ill-fare! Dead, forsook, cast off;
And none of you will bid the winter come
To thrust his icy fingers in my maw,
Nor let my kingdom's rivers take their course
Through my burn'd bosom, nor entreat the north
To make his bleak winds kiss my parched lips
And comfort me with cold. I do not ask you much;
I beg cold comfort; and you are so strait
And so ingrateful you deny me that.

Poisoned—bad food! Dead, forsaken, lost;
and none of you will ask the winter to come
and push his icy fingers into my mouth,
or let the rivers of my kingdom run through
my burning heart, nor ask the North
to send his harsh winds to kiss my parched lips
and comfort me with the cold. I'm not asking much
from you; I'm asking for cold comfort; and you are
so ungenerous
and so ungrateful that you won't let me have it.

PRINCE HENRY.
O that there were some virtue in my tears,
That might relieve you!

I wish that my tears had some power
to give you relief!

KING JOHN.
The salt in them is hot.
Within me is a hell; and there the poison
Is as a fiend confin'd to tyrannize
On unreprievable condemned blood.

The salt in them is hot.
There is a hell inside me; and the poison
is a devil put in there to attack
the unsaveable condemned blood.

Enter the BASTARD

BASTARD.
O, I am scalded with my violent motion
And spleen of speed to see your Majesty!

Oh, I am boiling with the rush I have had
to charge here to see your Majesty!

KING JOHN.
O cousin, thou art come to set mine eye!
The tackle of my heart is crack'd and burnt,
And all the shrouds wherewith my life should sail
Are turned to one thread, one little hair;

Oh cousin, you have come in time to close my eyes!
The ropes of my heart are cracked and burnt,
and all the sails that should drive my life
are hanging by one thread, a tiny hair;

My heart hath one poor string to stay it by,
Which holds but till thy news be uttered;
And then all this thou seest is but a clod
And module of confounded royalty.

BASTARD.
The Dauphin is preparing hitherward,
Where God He knows how we shall answer him;
For in a night the best part of my pow'r,
As I upon advantage did remove,
Were in the Washes all unwarily
Devoured by the unexpected flood.

[The KING dies]

SALISBURY.
You breathe these dead news in as dead an ear.
My liege! my lord! But now a king-now thus.

PRINCE HENRY.
Even so must I run on, and even so stop.
What surety of the world, what hope, what stay,
When this was now a king, and now is clay?

BASTARD.
Art thou gone so? I do but stay behind
To do the office for thee of revenge,
And then my soul shall wait on thee to heaven,
As it on earth hath been thy servant still.
Now, now, you stars that move in your right spheres,
Where be your pow'rs? Show now your mended faiths,
And instantly return with me again
To push destruction and perpetual shame
Out of the weak door of our fainting land.
Straight let us seek, or straight we shall be sought;
The Dauphin rages at our very heels.

SALISBURY.
It seems you know not, then, so much as we:
The Cardinal Pandulph is within at rest,
Who half an hour since came from the Dauphin,
And brings from him such offers of our peace
As we with honour and respect may take,
With purpose presently to leave this war.

BASTARD.
He will the rather do it when he sees

---

my heart has only one weak string left,
which is holding out only until I can hear your news;
and then what you see will just be a lump of earth,
a counterfeit of destroyed royalty.

The Dauphin is coming this way,
and only God knows how we will repel him;
in the night I lost the best part of my forces,
which I was taking the opportunity to move,
and in the Washes they were taken by surprise,
swept away by an unexpected flood.

You are telling this fatal news to a dead man.
My lord! My lord! Just now he was a king, now this.

That is how I must carry on, and how I will end.
what guarantee is there in the world, what hope, what support,
when this was once a king, and is now clay?

Have you gone? I am only remaining
to take revenge on your behalf,
and then my soul shall be your servant in heaven
as it still is on earth.
Now, you stars that are moving in your correct orbits,
where are your powers? Show me how you have returned to your loyalties,
and come back with me at once
to throw destruction and eternal shame
out of the weak door of our shrinking country.
Let us go hunting at once, or we shall be hunted;
the Dauphin is charging up behind us.

It seems that you don't know what we do:
Cardinal Pandulph is resting inside,
he came from the Dauphin half an hour ago,
and brings offers of peace from him
that we can accept honourably,
and will let us stop this war at once.

He will be more agreeable to peace terms

Ourselves well sinewed to our defence.

SALISBURY.
Nay, 'tis in a manner done already;
For many carriages he hath dispatch'd
To the sea-side, and put his cause and quarrel
To the disposing of the Cardinal;
With whom yourself, myself, and other lords,
If you think meet, this afternoon will post
To consummate this business happily.

BASTARD.
Let it be so. And you, my noble Prince,
With other princes that may best be spar'd,
Shall wait upon your father's funeral.

PRINCE HENRY.
At Worcester must his body be interr'd;
For so he will'd it.

BASTARD.
Thither shall it, then;
And happily may your sweet self put on
The lineal state and glory of the land!
To whom, with all submission, on my knee
I do bequeath my faithful services
And true subjection everlastingly.

SALISBURY.
And the like tender of our love we make,
To rest without a spot for evermore.

PRINCE HENRY.
I have a kind soul that would give you thanks,
And knows not how to do it but with tears.

BASTARD.
O, let us pay the time but needful woe,
Since it hath been beforehand with our griefs.
This England never did, nor never shall,
Lie at the proud foot of a conqueror,
But when it first did help to wound itself.
Now these her princes are come home again,
Come the three corners of the world in arms,
And we shall shock them. Nought shall make us rue,
If England to itself do rest but true.

Exeunt

when he sees us strongly prepared for our defence.

*No, it's almost done already;
he has sent many carriages down
to the coast, and left his negotiations
in the hands of the cardinal;
you and I and other lords,
if you agree, will meet with him this afternoon
to bring about a happy ending to this business.*

*I agree. And you, my noble Prince,
with the other princes who can best be spared,
will attend to the funeral of your father.*

*He must be buried at Worcester;
that's what he ordered.*

*He'll be taken there then;
your sweet self can happily assume
the title and rule of the country!
In all humilty I offer you on my knees
my faithful service,
and eternal loyalty.*

*And we all offer you the same love,
to be yours, pure, forever.*

*I have a kind soul that would like to thank you,
and only knows how to do it with tears.*

*Let's not waste time in excessive mourning,
as we have had so much of that to do already.
This England never has, and never will,
been subjugated by a conqueror,
except when it has first weakened itself.
Now that we are all united once again,
the whole world could attack us at once
and we would thrash them. We shall never have any regrets,
as long as England stays true to itself.*

Made in the USA
Columbia, SC
27 July 2021